Praise for Book of the Silenced

This family's journey reflects the courage required when medicine meets the unknown. Their persistence and faith in the face of an underappreciated stealth infection (neurobartonellosis) reminds us why scientific curiosity and human compassion must walk hand in hand.

Edward B. Breitschwerdt, DVM
Professor of Medicine and Infectious Diseases
North Carolina State University

Book of the Silenced is one of the most important medical memoirs of our time. It is an account of a family's nightmare inside a drug-oriented medical system in desperate need of reform, a system that brutalizes patients by treating symptoms instead of addressing the cause of disease. This should be required reading for every physician, nurse, medical student, administrator, policymaker, and parent. I commend this family for refusing to stay quiet.

John P. Monhollon
Founder and Medical Director of Florida Integrative Medical Center in Sarasota, Florida

~

This book is a clear-eyed and compassionate testament to what it means to love fiercely inside a healthcare system that too often forgets the human being at its center.

More than a memoir, Book of the Silenced is a quiet but powerful call to action. It reminds us that healing does not arise solely from protocols or productivity metrics, but from presence, relationship, and trust. In an era when medicine risks becoming an exercise in box-checking and billing optimization, this book argues persuasively for a return to something deeply human. It is essential reading for clinicians, administrators, and anyone who believes that medicine must remain, above all, an act of care.

Syed A. Asad, MD
Neurologist
Universal Neurological Care

~

This book bears witness to what happens when systems entrusted with healing cause harm, when parental instinct is dismissed, and when faith is tested in blood and breath. It draws the reader into the quiet violence of being unheard, the terror of loving a child inside a machine that refuses to listen, and the moral cost of enforced silence.

At its heart is Mikey—brilliant, gentle, and unbreakable—whose presence exposes every failure around him and whose endurance gives this story its lasting power.

Disturbing and necessary, Book of the Silenced lingers long after the final page, reshaping how we understand medicine, motherhood, and the courage required to stand when kneeling is demanded.

Shine on, Mikey.

Paula J. Sullivan, Esq.
Attorney at Law

Book of the Silenced

Gordana Smith

Book of the Silenced

ISBN: 979-8-9939110-1-4

Cover design by: Gordana Smith

Edited by: Danielle C. Tezcan

For permissions or inquiries, contact: phoenixrisespress@gmail.com

Scripture quotations are from the Holy Bible (NIV and other translations).

All author proceeds from this book are devoted to the care, advocacy, and future of the author's son, Mikey.

Disclaimer
This work is a piece of creative nonfiction based on my family's lived experiences, memories, and personal perceptions. Certain events, timelines, and details have been condensed, rearranged, or combined for narrative clarity, and some conversations have been reconstructed from memory. Names, identifying characteristics, locations, and institutional details have been changed, omitted, or fictionalized to protect privacy. Any resemblance to actual persons, living or dead, or to real organizations is coincidental or the result of these privacy measures.
The experiences described reflect our understanding and perceptions at the time and are not intended as factual findings or definitive statements about any individual, organization, or institution. Nothing in this book should be interpreted as an allegation, accusation, or assertion of wrongdoing against any person or entity.
This work is not intended to provide medical, psychological, legal, or other professional advice. The reflections and experiences shared are personal in nature and are not a substitute for professional consultation, diagnosis, or treatment.

First edition

Published by Phoenix Rises Press

Contents

Author's Note

There are books we choose to write.

And then there are books that choose us.

This one is the latter.

I didn't set out to write a memoir. I didn't want to be "that mother" with the blog, the binder of labs, the trauma turned manuscript. I just wanted my son to have a "normal" life. I wanted us to outlive the story, not relive it on paper.

But the silence grew teeth, and if I didn't speak, it would devour everything.

Some stories are shelved, others are shared. Ours refused the right to remain silent.

It is not just a record of what happened, but the echo of what tried to go unseen. It is about what breaks, what fights back, and what remains holy in the ruins.

A map made in darkness. A testimony built from the nights we almost gave up and the mornings we didn't.

I wrote this book between hospital beds and courtrooms, in moments borrowed from exhaustion, prayer, and waiting rooms where time no longer behaves. I wrote it in fragments, the way trauma teaches you to think:

Half-memories. Whispered prayers. Timestamped threats.

And miracles that never made it into a chart.

Every word you're about to read was wrestled for.

Every sentence cost something.

This is not just my story; it's a witness statement. A war journal, disguised as a book. And maybe, God willing, a weapon someone else can lift when their strength is gone.

If you are carrying pain you don't know how to name, faith that wavers, or hope you keep lowering so it will not disappoint you again, may these pages meet you where you are and remind you that you are not alone.

May love, in all its forms, endure in you too.

Let this book be a match you light and carry into your next dark moment and whisper:

I am not alone.

I am not crazy.

And I will not be silenced.

Dr. Gordana Smith (DAOM)

To My Mustache Man-

I thought I was the one saving you.
But you were the one who saved me.

Foreword

I have spent my career sitting with people in their darkest hours, listening to stories the world rarely hears. After a while, you start to believe there's little left that could shake you. Then you meet a child who proves you wrong.

I entered their lives first as a friend, and then as a counselor who came to care deeply for their son—our Mustache Man—as if he were my own.

I saw what was done to him inside a place that should have been safe, and I saw what it stole from him.

Those entrusted with his care made choices they could walk away from. He couldn't.

His parents should've protected him. They weren't allowed to.

The hospital discharge wasn't a finish line; it was the starting point of an even harder journey.

I sat beside this family during sleepless nights and impossible days when no one could say what might come next.

I watched a mother crumble to the floor in a chapel, her legs unable to carry the weight of what she feared might come. I saw a father carry his son not only through physical pain, but through a system that often looked past him as if he were invisible.

And I saw an innocent, trusting, pure child try to make sense of a world that suddenly made none.

There were moments I didn't know how they endured, until I saw something stronger than sorrow at work: grace taking root where grief should have settled, faith standing in a furnace where fear had every reason to win, and love becoming an act of holy defiance when everything else had already broken.

Most families would not survive what they did. Fewer still would choose to relive it in order to help others. Yet here they are, telling the truth not for attention, but for justice. For healing. Not just for Mikey, but for every child who has ever been lost in the cracks of a system that should have protected them. For the sake of others who can't find the strength—or safety—to say this truth out loud.

It asks *us* to look at what we'd rather ignore, and that's exactly why this book is necessary.

If you are a parent, this story will live in your bones.

If you work with children, it will hold a mirror to your hands.

If you hold power over another person's life, it will ask you to answer for it.

And it should.

I hope every reader remembers this as they turn these pages: Behind every hospital badge and clinical note, behind every treatment plan and institutional decision, there is a child asking the same silent question:

Can you still see me?

To have walked beside them, to know Mikey, whose joy runs deeper than sorrow and whose strength was never hardened by what he survived, is a gift I do not take lightly. I am so deeply moved by his resilience, his insight, his unguarded heart, and that smile—indescribable, grounded in several cultures, and somehow unmistakably his.

His life, forged in places few understand, has become a light to more people than he and his parents may ever fully know. To know his story is to be confronted with a profound truth: that great suffering can carve a path to even greater love.

I'm humbled to witness the impact his story will have on the world.

And so, before you begin, I offer you the prayer I have held for this family, and I offer it now, to you:

May God give you eyes to see what others overlook, strength to speak when silence is easier, wisdom to act with courage, and compassion that can hold another's pain without breaking.

May He bless every heart that reads these pages with clarity, hope, and faith that makes healing possible.

John "Jack" Jones, Jr., LMHC

Before I formed you in the womb I knew you, before you were born, I set you apart. — *Jeremiah 1:5 (NIV)*

The Morning He Didn't Come

People say heartbreak hits like thunder. Mine rolled off a plane, pushed through an airport crowd in a wheelchair and couldn't look me in the eye. Couldn't even smile at me.

August 2025. Orlando Airport

Oreo and I waited at the gate, helium balloons bobbing from his Emotional Support harness—some saying, "Welcome Home," a few were hearts, and others had mustaches on them (he never admitted he liked those, but they always made him smile). I even curled my hair, as if something beautiful on the outside could anchor what was breaking inside.

People *awwed* at our little welcome-home scene, parting around us like water, unaware of what was coming toward us through that stream of travelers. My Mustache Man was coming back from Ohio; a place we had hoped would finally figure things out and provide answers.

Larry came into frame like a familiar landmark, but the absence beside him sent fear straight through my spine. Mikey wasn't there. Then my eyes lowered and found him, in a wheelchair, Larry pushing him with a care that made my throat tighten.

The boy who used to sing before his feet hit the floor was slumped forward, eyes somewhere I couldn't follow. His head was shaved clean. Dried blood and stitches traced angry lines across his scalp like a map to something I wasn't allowed to know. His hands lay limp on the armrests, as if even lifting them cost too much.

Oreo recognized him right away and lunged forward toward his favorite human with the pure, trusting joy only dogs still believe in. Mikey lifted his hand to pet him, but the motion was slow, distant, almost like he wasn't sure what to do. Oreo's tail slowed, uncertain, his eyes flicking up to Mikey's face before settling into a worried whine. The handsome young man who left for Ohio was not the one coming home.

Not even mustache balloons could pull a smile from him. He looked straight through me. I told myself it was just exhaustion, just the flight, just something temporary.

"Hey, baby," I whispered, leaning in to give him his welcome-home kiss, one hand on Oreo's fur and the other gripping the balloon strings like they could hold us together. I waited for him to kiss me back like he had every day of his life.

"Once I sit in the car…" he said, barely above a whisper.

That was the first time in twenty-one years that he didn't kiss me right away.

It stung more than I expected.

My forehead and cheeks ached in places his lips didn't find.

My eyes kept searching for his, hoping for some glimmer of recognition, but he stared past me like I was a stranger in a crowd. Ohio took something from him that did not make the return trip.

I smiled anyway. I stayed cheerful. Light. Practiced.

My face kept lying for both of us, but my eyes couldn't.

So, I held the balloons tighter, as if string and helium

alone could tether my boy to the world that was slipping away from him.

~

The Prophecy

May 20, 2020. 95 days after his 16th birthday.

Starlight Children's Hospital, Central Florida

The hospital air felt charged, as if the walls themselves had overheard his fear.

"Mama… something bad is about to happen. Really bad."

I turned toward him, my voice steady though his words iced through me.

"Nothing bad will happen to you. Mom and Dad are here. The staff is highly trained. You're safe."

But his eyes didn't soften. His tone sharpened, weighted with a gravity no child should ever have to hold.

"Mom," he said, slow like a funeral bell, "I *know* something bad is about to happen."

I tried humor—the armor I always reached for when fear tried to take the room.

"Well," I said, forcing a smile, "they'd have to get through Mama Bear first, and you know how that ends."

No smile. Only a sorrowful frustration that belonged to someone far older than sixteen.

"Mama… you don't understand. Something bad *will* happen. I saw it. Please don't let them hurt me. Please."

That word—*please*—broke something in me. Then came *the* look, but not that one of a child; eyes too ancient, searching. Gentle and sad all at once, as if he were begging me to step into a knowing I didn't yet possess. He was my son, my only child, yet in that moment he seemed a thousand years old.

And then–against his nature–tears began to fall.

Mikey rarely cried, but when he did, the world tilted. His tears came with a sound he couldn't stop, and the ache they left had nowhere to go. I pressed my cheek to his and whispered prayers, tangled with the fear that loving him might not be enough.

I didn't understand what he was trying to show me, I only knew I couldn't stop the dread rising inside me. Deep down—though I fought it with everything I had—I felt it, too.

That was the moment I started asking the question that would haunt every day that followed: What is the cost of knowing too soon?

I would spend the next five years trying to convince the world he had seen something real.

Belief, as it turned out, was more dangerous than knowing.

What followed wasn't just a season; it was an unending winter we were about to walk into together.

Part I: Ashes to Beauty

Chapter 1

Careless Tomorrows

B*efore the sky fell, the first rule of childhood was simple: apricots tasted better when they were stolen, and every spanking that followed was a sermon.*

My knees were always scraped, my curls always wild, and summers smelled like cut grass and bread cooling on windowsills. If playing carried us too far from home, we would slip into the closest friend's house and make ourselves guests. Neighbors gave us water when we were thirsty, sliced bread with jam when we were hungry, and a tug on the ear if we misbehaved while our parents weren't close enough to see. That was what belonging looked like then.

The alleys were our stadiums.

"That's five goals for me!" a boy shouted.

"Five? You couldn't score five even if the ball was tied to your shoe."

"At least I don't kick like your grandma."

"My grandma plays better than you."

The ball was half-flat, the score changed with every argument, and we didn't care. Dust in our mouths, laughter in our throats. Life felt careless then, as if tomorrow would always come.

Tomorrow did come—but it wasn't careless anymore.

No one told us the war was coming.

Chapter 2

Bread and Bombs

The war in Bosnia, part of the violent breakup of the former Yugoslavia, wasn't just about borders: It was about identity, ethnicity, and the terrifying speed with which neighbors became enemies.

April 1992. Yugoslavia

What do you do when the ground you stand on disappears? I was standing, but the country beneath me was not.

Neighbors we once shared bread with now looked past us like we were strangers. Or worse. "Don't wave," my mother whispered once, gripping my arm. "Waves can be mistaken for choosing sides."

When the sirens wailed and bombs shook our city, we pressed into basements like cattle in the cold, packed into the moldy guts of buildings while war roared above us, trying but unable to divide us.

Yet.

Food was scarce, and if you were lucky enough to eat every day, it was usually a can of eat-at-your-own-risk expired ingredients. We passed around dented tins like communion, scraping the bottom and pretending not to notice that beans tasted like metal and despair. Grief was detonating in places we hadn't yet learned to grieve. There was always someone with a guitar, a song daring to rise above the shaking walls, and the clink of tin openers undoing the same dinner. Again.

Always again.

"How long do these little brown bullets last?" someone asked, rolling a can between his palms.

"Longer than countries," someone else muttered.

The whole basement cracked up, nervous laughter ricocheting off the walls, louder than the shelling outside.

Laughter was like medicine: We overdosed when we had to.

I was twenty-one, old enough to know the world should've felt wider by then. My friends in other countries were cramming for exams, chasing first jobs, carelessly falling in and out of love. Me? I was in a basement, listening to endless fart jokes, wondering if laughter alone could hold despair at bay long enough for us to pretend the future was still out there, waiting.

At night, boots echoed across empty streets, and that sound told us everything we didn't want to know.

When the war came, it kicked the door off the hinges. It stayed, and it unpacked like an uninvited guest who refused to leave. Once it made itself at home, it rewrote every page of what life was supposed to be.

Even love.

Love in the Fire

Fall 1992. Bosnia

He was an Eagle Scout with a guitar, and I was his volleyball girl who wore innocence like perfume. We were too young to know the difference between forever and borrowed time, but old enough to feel the ache of a world burning down around us. There was no time for dreams when bombs fell like prophecies, and the air turned thick with smoke and shattered hopes.

"Do you think we'll make it out?" I whispered, though I wasn't sure if I meant the night or the war. Or just the fragile thread tying our names together.

He squeezed my hand tighter. "We'll make it. Even if the world burns down, we'll still be us."

But even as he said it, the walls rattled with another blast. Outside, the sky flickered red like God Himself had bled into the horizon and wasn't done yet.

Not knowing what time we had left, we eloped into the fire, hoping love would spare us. It didn't.

The very next day, shrapnel tore through his flesh, piercing through everything we hadn't lived yet. I became a nurse before I fully became a bride, measuring antibiotics and sorrow in equal parts. I changed his dressings at home (hospitals were overcrowded) while the television screen scrolled fresh death tolls across the bottom—a relentless tally of loss that never stopped climbing.

And as I tended his wounds, the earth opened for three graves:

—one for his younger brother,

—one for his father,

—one for our marriage.

Grief arrived faster than love had time to bloom.

The Curse of Expectation

In the Balkans, a childless marriage was never just a sorrow. It was a scandal. And always—always—it was the woman's fault.

My in-laws wanted an heir, and when no child came, they had a word for me that doesn't translate into English. (And thank God it doesn't!) I carried that word like a curse.

His wound made intimacy impossible, but I stubbornly believed that somehow—against biology and common sense

—I could conceive. I prayed knowing that the path to the altar could also be the path to my death.

I fasted not because food was lacking (though often it was), but because my longing demanded sacrifice. I lit candles until the wax burned my fingertips, as if their flicker could keep my heart from breaking.

Alas, no child came.

The war ended in 1996, but not all the casualties were bodies to be buried and mourned…my dream of parenting withered and died, an invisible victim of war.

Eventually, we divorced. No fights, no courts. Just two souls releasing each other gently, like birds back into a sky neither of us trusted anymore.

He let me go. I let him go.

We never spoke of the child we couldn't have.

Exile Within Exile

Fall 1998. Bosnia

Loss was nothing new to me; I had watched war erase faces, futures, entire cities. But divorce was a stranger of its own, a loss that kept living.

At twenty-seven, my marriage ended. The boy I'd grown up with, loved since high school, married during war and then unspooled from, became a stranger overnight. It felt like walking through familiar rooms with all the doors suddenly locked.

I worked as a linguist for high-ranking American officers, assigned to peacekeeping missions across the region. A job transfer to another city came just in time, when our hometown had become too small for the ghosts of us.

Peacekeeping sometimes meant promoting the dialogue between warring sides, or when diplomacy failed, to deliver thinly veiled threats. We sat across from local officials in ruined buildings and tried to stitch up wounds with the language of treaties.

"Gotcha," one general said, in agreement.

He meant "Understood."

The interpreters cringed; the locals smiled politely—but not for the reasons he thought. In our language, *"gotcha"* sounds like underwear.

It wasn't that the talks weren't serious. It's just hard to feel the gravity of peace when it ends in panties.

But peacekeeping is not always peace.

I saw things no one should ever have to witness—mass graves, hollowed-out villages, children born of violence, fathered by war. Foreign soldiers arrived with steel and arrogance, marching through our grief as if it were a training ground. Some tried to make friends by handing out candy, as if sugar could sweeten rubble. Children walked barefoot past tanks, clutching candy from soldiers they did not trust—their eyes never leaving the helmets and guns. Fear was muscle memory, even in the smallest hands.

Back home, I became a stranger in my own story. I had worn the uniform of the West—of those who had bombed us.

Even my uncle who taught me to ride a bike shook his head and whispered, "You've forgotten who you are."

He muttered it softly, like a prayer—but it struck like a gavel. Sentence delivered.

Too Western for the East. Too Eastern for the West. Exiled from both.

And so—love? That was something I no longer allowed myself to believe in.

Especially not with an American.

Least of all with an American officer.

Chapter 3

God's Irony

I *didn't mean to laugh. Okay, maybe I did. But in my defense, he was the one who sat in the chocolate milk—what was I supposed to do?*

Fall 2001. Bosnia

God, in His favorite kind of irony, sent me *that* man. Larry.

An American officer I never wanted and never imagined I could love. Quiet, brooding, tightly wound like a man built from rules. Still bleeding from betrayals I hadn't yet asked about.

Our first encounter was… memorable—though probably not in the way you're thinking. In Bosnia, where laughter was scarce and grief was the daily currency, our first meeting still managed to be unforgettable.

The klutz of my life was running late for his assignment; the convoy lined up waiting for him. His soldiers had set a trap—or maybe they cared, I'll never know—leaving a chocolate milk right on the seat for their officer. He came rushing in, all business, no time to look. He sat.

SPLAT.

Chocolate milk exploded everywhere. His immaculate

uniform pants looked like they'd survived a toddler's birthday party gone wrong. Time froze. The soldiers went dead quiet, like the silence after a grenade pin hits the ground.

"WHO left this here?!" he barked, springing up, pants dripping.

Not a sound. Not a breath. You could hear buttons sweating on their uniforms.

And me? I laughed so hard I could barely breathe, and every attempt to compose myself made it worse. He sat there in wet, brown-stained pants, glaring at me like he might self-combust on the spot. The soldiers risked a glance at me that said, *lady, you're gonna die*, but I couldn't help myself.

He turned toward me—slowly. A statue come to life. His jaw clenched. Daggers flying from his eyes.

"Are you quite finished?" he snapped.

I shook my head, tears streaming. "Not even close."

He glared. I cackled. His men held their breath like witnesses to a duel. He stood there, pants soaked, dignity murdered, and I knew—I had made an enemy. If looks could kill, Bosnia would have lost one more civilian that day.

But for the first time in years, I remembered what it was to laugh without permission. Totally worth it.

I don't remember exactly when I stopped thinking he was emotionally constipated; but one day, the silences between us weren't so sharp and the walls we'd built held doors we didn't slam shut as quickly.

Body Betrayed Me

Spring 2002. Bosnia

Just as love began to bloom, my body quietly turned against me.

It started slowly, like ink bleeding into water—creeping outward until everything it touched was stained.

Years of walking through bombed-out streets where even the air was poison.

Years of carrying the weight of stories too heavy for a single soul.

Years of silencing grief, because survival never left room for it.

It all lived in me. Until one day, it didn't. My body was too tired to carry it anymore.

The doctor said it with a voice soft, but final. "Your kidneys are failing."

I sat still, hands folded tightly in my lap, as if obedience might save me."Is there any hope?"

He shook his head. Slowly.

How do you tell a woman—just thirty-one years old—who's already buried her innocence, her home, her marriage, bodies in unmarked graves; who's stood in cities lit by fire instead of electricity, that *this* is what will finally undo her? Not yet. Not like this…

The year that followed was a blur of needles, silent nights, and questions too heavy to name. I watched my hair fall in clumps, my strength with it. I lost my job, my identity, sight of the woman I thought I was.

"Nothing else we can do," echoed.

And then—

Where medicine failed, faith did not. It didn't fix me, but it didn't leave me, either. I refused to let this be the end of my story *(as if I had any say in it).*

My motherland abandoned me, and my body carried the story of what was lost.

But my soul?

It remembered who it belonged to—and it sang.

Chapter 4

The Pilgrimage

B*lessed are those whose strength is in You, whose hearts are set on pilgrimage. — Psalm 84:5 (NIV)*

May 2003. Saint Basil of Ostrog monastery in Montenegro

Every pilgrimage begins with an ending. Mine began at the end of myself, where medicine stepped back and hope spoke a dialect I couldn't translate. As an interpreter, I gave language to other people's pain, but had none left for my own.

I didn't hear a voice from heaven that day. Just a whisper, a nudge maybe.

As my hair began to grow back, the whisper returned too, like breath surfacing after being held too long beneath the water. By May, I knew I had to go somewhere holy, not to escape my brokenness, but to meet God in it.

"Are you *sure* you want to do this, it's very a long drive?" Larry asked softly.

I met his eyes and nodded.

Some places demand our brokenness before they can offer peace: they ask us to kneel before we can stand again. And when your feet no longer want to move, faith sometimes walks without them.

A Night Beneath Eternity

We slept on gravel beneath that vast sky, surrounded by strangers whose lives brushed against ours for a single night. On top of that mountain, I felt overwhelming peace that seeped through every ache and every scar, settling deep into my bones.

At four in the morning, we woke without an alarm, guided only by the silence that felt alive. Larry and I found each other's hands in the dark and prayed in that unspoken language only God understands.

Larry had not grown up with God, yet he stood beside me that morning with a sincerity that asked for nothing and gave everything.

We were already engaged, but I had never told him the truth that pressed against my soul: that I loved him enough to let him go. It felt kinder to let him lose me now than to ask him to carry my grave inside his chest.

And so, he stayed, quiet and steady. With *me.*

Encountering the Holy

Later that morning, when the crowds thinned, we entered the chamber that held Saint Basil's relics. Its narrow and short doorway forces you to remember the oldest truth—we are lifted only when we learn to bow low.

I had no polished prayer, no eloquent words to offer, and my faith wasn't tidy. My body was broken, my spirit exhausted. I just knelt there, forehead against cool stone, and whispered from the rawest part of my soul:

"God… if there is still life in me… let it be used for something holy."

I think that's where He met me: in the silence, after I stopped trying to make sense of it.

I walked out of that chamber with a quiet knowing that my story wasn't finished.

Chapter 5

Happy Birthday, Soldier

W*e lit 33 candles and sang Happy Birthday off-key in three languages.*

June 2003. Bosnia

He looked so happy that day, laughing with cake on his fingers, making me promise next year would be even better. I smiled, nodded, kissed him like I meant forever.

But something had already… changed in me.

I was convinced I was dying. The tests, the waiting, the ache that never went away. I told myself it would be kinder to push him away now than to let him watch me fade. I couldn't marry him only to make him a widower. I began to suggest gently that he go back to the States; never as a goodbye, only as a next step. I told him we needed a place to settle, somewhere quiet and green. I asked him to find it for us, hoping it would give him something to hold onto when I no longer could.

A home. A future I had no intention of joining.

He didn't want to go. He fought me on it for days, said we should leave together. Said nothing mattered if we were side by side. But my stubborn Balkan head, always holding the line, wouldn't budge.

So, there we were, at the airport. I stood frozen, arms folded tight, heart louder than the boarding calls. Larry beside me, suitcase at his feet, eyes searching my face for something I couldn't give. He exhaled, a sound that seemed to carry the weight of a thousand things unsaid.

"You sure?" he asked.

I nodded, not trusting myself to speak.

He took a breath. Held it for a moment. "I love you enough," he whispered, "to hate every second of this."

"I love you, too," I said. "Sometimes!"

He grinned.

Then I let go.

He walked toward security without turning back. My legs wouldn't move. My heart already had. The sound of rolling suitcases and distant chatter blurred to nothing. All that was left was the ghost of his warmth on my skin… and the silence he left behind.

And when he was gone, I let the weight of it all settle. I had sent away the only man who ever made me feel safe, and I surrendered to whatever time I had left.

But then came July

July 28, 2003. Bosnia

My sister had a routine gynecologist appointment and asked me to go with her. I resisted—what was the point? I had walked those hallways before, listened to the cold finality of medical voices, and I didn't need another reminder.

But she insisted.

After her exam, she looked at me and said, "Your turn."

"What am I, your emotional support goat?"

"Yes. Now bleat and get on the table."

(God really knew I needed her with me that day.)

I laughed, half-annoyed, and climbed reluctantly onto the table.

"Knock yourself out," I told the doctor, joking to cover the sting I thought I'd feel.

The familiar room was dim. The screen glowed faintly as the doctor moved the wand across my stomach. It was the same doctor I had seen years ago, back when I was with my ex. The office hadn't changed. Same worn chair, same colorless walls, same sense of failure still clinging to the air. Back then, the conversations had been about what my body couldn't do.

Now, here we were.

The doctor paused, his hand hovering. His eyes moved from the image to my face.

"You're not supposed to be able to do this," he said.

"Well, tell it to my God…" I managed to say.

After a moment he said, "You're about ten weeks pregnant."

It was like watching a TV with the volume off. I could see his lips moving, but I had *no* idea what he was saying. It felt like someone else's news. I sat there, still half-draped in that paper sheet, wondering if the silence in my head meant I was in shock or finally, finally at peace.

I heard my sister squeal from the waiting room. That eavesdropper always managed to make me laugh.

And then I heard it. A soft, steady, impossibly certain sound.

A heartbeat.

Not mine.

Joy and disbelief were so tightly wound together, I couldn't tell one from the other.

Pregnant.

Me?

~

I barely remember the drive home.

We didn't say much at first, both still stunned. My sister kept giving me that mischievous look, raising her eyebrows like she was holding in a scream until we both lost it. That's how we've always been: feeding off each other's laughter.

Tears, too.

She reached over, squeezed my hand, and said, "You're still my emotional support goat." Then, a smirk: "I hope you know I'd bleat for you, too."

I laughed through tears I didn't know were coming, as if I knew I'd learn soon enough that miracles do not close a story.

They open one.

Chapter 6

Promise of the Promised Land

People said the healthcare here was the best in the world. I didn't need the best—I just needed enough to keep my baby safe. But even that was too much to ask.

August 2003. Florida

When he learned about the baby, Larry's light turned into contagious radiance; joy made the air around us softer, as if the world had shifted to make space for a new beginning. He had already uprooted everything from Indiana and found us a little place in Florida, saying the sun and the sea air would be good for my health.

We started poor but happy.

We had little more than borrowed furniture, mismatched dishes, and hand-me-down clothes pressed into our hands by strangers' kindness. But the crib was brand new. The sheets were white and crisp, as if we were preparing for something sacred. Some nights I lay awake beneath the thin light spilling through the blinds, wondering if love alone could be enough, if joy could bloom in soil so bare.

For a moment, it felt like enough.

A bright future was waiting, or so I wanted to believe. The

doctors were better, I heard. The health care would be better, I thought.

It all sounded like safety, and I was a fool to believe it.

The Day You Came

February 2004. Florida: The year God broke the rules

That February morning, my water broke.

My fingers trembled as I called Riverbend Medical Center, my voice steady only because fear hadn't fully taken root yet. Their replies were flat and rehearsed.

"It's probably just a mucus plug. Wait for contractions."

I didn't even get the chance to say that *every* drop was gone.

While we waited for contractions that weren't coming, Larry took me to the library knowing the scent of worn pages was my favorite in the world; the smell of safety, of escape, of something solid when life wasn't. I thought nothing could ever replace it.

Until I smelled you, Mikey.

Your *baba* was visiting, and when she heard what happened—the calls, the dismissal, the waiting—her arms flew up in wild disbelief, her voice breaking in jagged English:

"They crazy! That's baby water! You sit here why? We go *now*!"

If she could've tucked me under her arm like a loaf of bread and marched me in herself, she would have. She didn't wait for a second opinion and thank God she didn't.

"No contractions?"

The nurse didn't even glance up from her chart.

"It's probably just mucus. First-time moms panic over everything."

My voice cracked sharper than I meant it to.

"I'm not panicking. My water broke."

She finally looked up, eyes flat.

"Honey, if your water broke, you wouldn't be standing here."

I stared at her, biting down on words only war survivors know how to swallow. They nearly missed the miracle altogether. But this time, we refused to be ignored.

"I don't feel heard. I'd like to speak with your supervisor. Now, please."

When they finally checked, panic.

I hadn't lost some water; I had lost all of it. You had been drifting for over fifteen hours in a sea that had vanished. Human error brushing up against something holy. But you made it.

This was only the first time you survived what never should've happened in the first place.

A Name Older Than Time

I didn't scream during those thirty-six hours of labor. No swearing, no throwing things, no threats to Larry's life—though he deserved a few, just for breathing too loudly.

And then—*you.*

There was a moment of silence long enough for my mind to fill in every terrible possibility. I frantically scanned the room—faces, hands, movements—trying to read something, anything, before someone said a word. *I remembered this exact moment twenty years later…*

Then I heard it: your first cry.

A small, raw sound of your lungs figuring out how to be lungs. I hadn't realized I'd been holding my breath until I heard yours.

They placed you in Larry's arms first. I watched my husband, my steady, quiet soldier, come undone. His shoulders shook. His breath caught. And when he finally found his voice, it cracked wide open:

"He's okay. He's alive. He's normal."

The words tumbled out, part prayer, part promise, a moment too vast for language.

Then he placed you in my arms. And oh—

The weight of you was somehow the heaviest and the lightest thing I'd ever carried.

My arms could hold you, but my heart could barely contain you. I traced the outline of your tiny face—your perfect mouth, tiny little fingers, every impossible piece of you—and whispered *thank yous* I couldn't string together into sentences.

We named you Michael Gabriel.

Two archangels folded into one name. Sword and trumpet. Warrior and messenger. Heaven and earth. You were not here because science permitted it, or because doctors explained it.

You were here because God remembered me.

But your story, my son, didn't begin with us.

It started way before your father cried in the delivery room. Long before I labored through pain and fear and joy to bring you into the world or ever knew how to pray your name.

You weren't just born. You were delivered.

Not only from me, but through me.

Whatever you grow to become—prophet or poet, healer or dreamer, or simply beautifully and wholly yourself—you will always be the miracle I was told would never come.

The war I survived and the endurance it forged in me? It became the weapon I would one day lift to fight for my cradled miracle.

And so began the quiet years, those small, ordinary days when my miracle learned how to walk, to speak, to ask why.

In more than one language, and clear as a bell.

Chapter 7

Where the Bells Still Ring

T*he sound of distant church bells in Belgrade cut through the twilight air; clear, steady, and haunting.*

March 2006. Belgrade (Serbia)

Mikey's hands found ours as he looked up, eyes wide with wonder.

"Daddy, look! The clouds are painting."

Larry knelt beside him, worn and quiet, his gaze tracing the streaks of pink and gold that stretched across the bruised sky.

"They are, curly," he whispered, soft enough that only we could hear. "Just for you."

I watched them there—father and son—one who had seen too much, one who had only just begun to learn what the world could hold.

When Larry deployed to Afghanistan in 2005, just after Mikey's first birthday, I had no family nearby. No tribe. Just my boy and my prayers. We uprooted and moved to Belgrade; the same city American planes had bombed just years before. But we weren't there for politics. We were there for love.

Surrounded by cousins, kissed by grandmothers, running barefoot through courtyards where laughter drowned out the memory of sirens, Mikey couldn't help but thrive.

When Larry's deployment ended, he joined us; he had come from another battlefield, but somehow this broken city felt like an oasis. However, even in Belgrade, the past found ways to whisper through the noise of the streets. Larry would flinch at motorcycles, firecrackers, even the ringing bells—echoes of places where fear had taken root.

One afternoon, as the bells tolled longer than usual, Mikey clapped in delight. Larry didn't; he watched, his eyes distant, waiting for ghosts no one else could see.

That night, in the quiet of our room, his voice broke the silence.

"It's strange," he said softly, almost to himself. "How a place once burning feels safer than home."

I didn't ask what he'd seen in the desert, I already knew too much.

But Mikey didn't.

To him, the sky was still a canvas of hope and color.

Another evening, as the light bled into the horizon, Mikey pointed up again. "Did they paint for you in the desert, Daddy?"

Larry hesitated, his eyes tracing the fading pink and orange.

"Sometimes," he said, his voice quiet. "But it was harder to see."

"Why?" Mikey asked.

"Because I didn't have you there to show me."

The bells rang on—both invitation and warning that even Heaven's gifts can be dragged through fire.

And fire was coming.

Chapter 8

Old City Welcomed an Old Soul

The time in Belgrade stitched us together in ways I didn't fully understand until much later. But time does what time always does—it pulls you forward, ready or not.

Spring 2007. Florida

Orders came, goodbyes were whispered, and the next chapter waited across an ocean in Mikey's hometown where history clung to every street corner. The salt air and wide skies of St. Augustine had been patiently waiting for us to come back.

We spent endless hours by the sea. He'd learned to swim in the Adriatic Sea, but it was the Atlantic that taught him courage. Wave after wave, he charged forward—fearless, grinning, saltwater clinging to his lashes, laughter cutting through the roar of the surf.

My Curly Covenant

I never asked for a sign, only for peace. Instead, I was given a boy and learned that peace isn't free. It asks everything of you.

His wild curls had a mind of their own, falling across his chocolate-smudged cheeks like a crown tilted by mischief. He'd puff at them like a tiny firefighter on a mission, his smile lingering like sunlight long after the day was gone.

After sun-soaked days that left his skin kissed by salt and laughter, he'd sneak barefoot into the kitchen, sticky and humming some silly tune he probably just made up. The smell of the sea and childhood followed him.

"What's for dinner, Mama?"

"Beans," I'd say. "Your favorite."

"Yum."

His little finger would sneak toward the pot, then jerk back before the wooden spoon could catch him.

"Buddy," I'd laugh, "go shower and change. You're still wearing half the ocean."

He'd backpedal, eyes still on the pot.

"I'll be fast," he'd promise. "Don't let the beans start without me."

He'd grin—rule dodged, game on—then collapse on the couch.

"Just resting my eyes," he'd mumble, and be out cold before I could turn around, curls still damp with seawater and dreams. Swimsuit and all.

It was the ordinary moments like this one that made our home feel safe, before the past found its way back into my kitchen. I once hated beans: their metallic taste reminded me of rationed years, of basements and borrowed time.

But Mikey changed that.

With him, beans became supper softened by garlic and laughter. The flavor of survival turned into the flavor of grace. Love does that sometimes… redeems the taste of old sorrows and turns what once kept you alive into something worth living for.

In those evenings, when I lifted him from the couch and felt his weight surrender to my arms, it was more than love I carried. It was a promise, quiet and whole, asking to be believed.

Years later, when the charts thickened and the questions multiplied, I wrestled with the cruel arithmetic of miracles:

Why would a miracle come only to later cause suffering?

Was he given as punishment… or purpose?

Chapter 9

Don't Mind Me, I'm Just Growing Up

Animals would choose him. Strangers would notice. And life would begin asking more of him than it ever should from a child.

2007. St. Augustine

The first time I realized my son wasn't quite ordinary, he was three years old and negotiating Christmas like a seasoned philosopher.

"Mikey, what would you like us to get you this year for Christmas?"

He grinned that mischievous grin and answered without hesitation: "I really would like an older brother!"

I laughed and pressed, "Uhm… What else can we get you?"

He paused, eyes dancing. "A kitten?"

I smiled. "We can work with that."

So that Christmas, his third one, home came not one—but two kittens—the cutest little fluffballs he named Tigger and Snuggles.

My Mustache Man always loved animals, and if I didn't know better, I could swear he could talk to them. Not in the usual boyhood way—frogs in pockets, lizards cupped in muddy hands; he seemed to speak to them.

There was something otherworldly in the way furry creatures recognized him.

~

One summer in Greece—one of many—while Larry and I marveled at ruins of ancient faith, strangers began smiling and pointing at Mikey. He was five.

I held his little hand, but when I turned, I nearly stumbled: four or five stray cats had fallen into line behind him, padding along as if he carried an invisible leash of grace. We chuckled. He just shrugged.

People passing by took pictures, but to him, it was the most natural thing in the world.

He crouched beside one of the cats, as if picking up a conversation they'd started in another life. Honestly, if one of them had spoken back, I wouldn't have been surprised.

One cat lingered in the shadows, watching him with the calm certainty of something that had already chosen him.

Gainfully Deployed (Again)

When Larry deployed again in 2009—his third deployment in eight years, this time to Africa—Mikey missed him fiercely.

At soccer games and school performances, I saw it: that quiet flicker of sadness when other boys' dads filled the stands. In those moments, I had to be both mother and father. I clapped louder. Hugged tighter. Loved for two. My son refused to fold under the weight.

He rose.

By kindergarten, Mikey was devouring Harry Potter, his tiny finger tracing each line like a scholar of magic.

He enjoyed playing chess with my father like he was born for it; they would sit across from each other, elbows on the table, eyes locked on the board like soldiers in negotiations. The room smelled like strong coffee and quiet judgment.

"You know," Mikey said, eyeing the board, "this game would be over by now if you didn't take six years per move."

My father didn't look up. "Chess is a game of patience."

"So is being your opponent."

Just then, *deda's* phone rang—one of his cousins from the old country. The call lasted a whole three seconds before the volume doubled.

Mikey didn't even flinch.

"Why is everyone yelling?"

I yelled from the kitchen. "They're *not* yelling. They're talking."

Eyeroll.

Whether it was knights or queens, spells or soccer balls, Mikey was never lukewarm—he was always all in.

Church Love

He *loved* God like some kids love roller coasters—wildly, eagerly, with a wide-eyed wonder that made faith look effortless. He loved the incense, the Byzantine chants, the sacred quiet. Church wasn't an obligation to him; it was home.

For all his reverence, he was still just a boy who loved the world in simple ways: soccer and basketball, frogs and grasshoppers, grilled corn in the summer.

And he held his childhood crushes like sacred secrets.

One girl in particular—Nadia, the quiet, soft-eyed girl from church—had owned his heart since the day they met. When years later she started having seizures, Mikey whispered to me one night, voice barely audible in the dark:

"I wish I could take it instead, so she could be healthy."

That was Mikey: willing to carry someone else's cross… even if the weight of it broke him.

For now, the weight of it will only scratch the surface.

Chapter 10

The Kitten

S*ome children learn early what hurts. Mikey learned who.*

Summer, 2018. Bosnia (before high school)

That half-dead, wild, maggot-filled little thing would've made most kids look away.

Not Mikey.

He dropped to his knees like he was picking up something sacred. The kitten scratched him in its panic, in the chaos of rescue. His hand bled, but he didn't even flinch, just kept holding it…never knowing what had passed between them.

"What in the world, Mikey!? Bare hands? Open skin? You think you're some kind of… saint for strays? *Bože me sačuvaj! (God save us. The Balkan reflex to every catastrophe, great or small.).*

He blinked up at me, wide-eyed, the picture of wounded innocence, holding the tiny shaking thing like a treasure.

"It scratched me a little, but—"

"A little?! Look at your hand, you're bleeding!" I yelled, dabbing the wound with *patoka*, weaker alcohol from my dad's moonshine experiments we used for everything from a pimple, to dusting, to cleaning wounds with it.

"Ow—okay, okay, okay—"

"You don't touch bleeding animals! You don't touch anything bleeding unless you're wearing gloves and a hazmat suit!" I hissed through my teeth. "What if it had rabies? What if it had—what if—"

I stopped. My breath caught in my throat like a bone. *I* was doing it.

I was her. My mother.

Mikey stared at me with those ridiculous puppy eyes, making it impossible to stay mad at that face. I sat down beside him, threw my arm over his shoulder, and sighed.

"Let me tell you the story of why your butt isn't sore right now.

When I was about five, I fell off my bike and skinned my knees so bad you'd have thought I was attacked by a bear. Blood was pouring down my legs like Niagara Falls, and in my tiny, overly dramatic brain, I was definitely dying. I even started rehearsing my final words.

When she heard me cry, my mama came flying out of the house, apron still tied around her waist, flour up to her elbows like she'd just been dragged out of a bag of dough. She was screaming like I'd been shot, barefoot and bolting down the road like it was the end of days.

Then she saw me sitting there—alive, conscious, very much *not dying*, and the switch flipped. Her panic turned to pure Balkan fury. Without missing a beat, she grabbed me like a sack of potatoes, and with one hand on my ear and the other pointing to the sky, she started shouting about "scaring her to death" and "what will the neighbors think."

And yes, she spanked my little butt all the way inside. I limped in like a war veteran and never rode that bike again… at least not until I figured out how to fall without turning it into a Shakespearean tragedy.

That was the day I learned: in Bosnia, you don't die dramatically in peace—you get punished for it first."

"Don't scare me like that again!" she'd shouted.

"I never understood it then. But I do now. That's love, curly. Terrified love. Now give me that mutant street cat before you lose another limb. We'll take him to the vet first thing in the morning," I promised.

He smiled.

The kitten didn't make it through the night, but the scratch did. My mother's intuition *knew*, heartache arrived on silent paws.

Later, we'd learn that the kitten carried Bartonella—an invisible thief that would hijack his body, his mind, his future.

His beautiful, beautiful brain.

It didn't strike right away. First, that scratch slept.

Then, it waited.

Then—it changed everything.

Forever.

Chapter 11

Scroll and Sword

Every soul enters the world with two witnesses by their side, carrying two things unseen. A scroll to read, and a sword to lift. One holds the promise. The other defends it.

The day I first held *you*, I saw the distant knowing in your eyes, the look of someone who'd already glimpsed the other side of mercy and made peace with the cost.

You stared at me as if you recognized the mission and forgave me in advance for not understanding it yet.

The nurse said, "Here he is."

But I knew better. You weren't arriving. You were returning.

Years later, darkness would come wearing medical badges and clinical words.

The same hands that once cradled you would steady IV lines, sign court papers, and lift prayers heavy enough to bruise the heavens.

Your war was about to begin, and I would remember for both of us:

Your scroll would be written in test results. Your sword—in every word I spoke to protect you.

Part II: Into the Wilderness

What came before was the inheritance, a lineage of endurance written into our bones.

But what came next was the reckoning, when centuries of silence collided with my Miracle Child's cry in a hospital room, begging me not to let them hurt him.

The unseen war was never left in the past. It followed us into hospitals, into sleepless nights, into a future none of us could control.

This wasn't history anymore:
It was now.
It was us.
Survival in real time.

Chapter 12

Careful What You Pray For

The last time I saw my family as I once knew them was the summer of 2018. That year was golden, and we didn't know we were walking through the last chapter of before.

We laughed loudly in foreign streets, ate like we were invincible, chased sunsets like they belonged to us. Mikey and I were untethered, surrounded by family, friends, and food that made you close your eyes and hum.

Europe unfolded before us like a love letter—Bosnia, Serbia, Croatia, Montenegro. Sunsets in Santorini, storms rolling in over Lake Geneva, the way bread tasted like a sacred offering in a country that wasn't ours but welcomed us anyway.

In Switzerland, we climbed mountains and sat at the feet of peaks older than empires. But we also checked out chocolate-temptress places, because apparently, that's a law there.

Mikey stopped in front of one window like he'd just seen the Holy Grail dipped in ganache.

"Mama," he whispered, "that chocolate looks like it has a financial advisor."

He leaned closer to the glass. "That one's wearing a bowtie," he said. "Pretty sure it just raised its monocle at me."

We went in: everything gleamed like jewelry on velvet. Mikey chose one tiny, absurdly expensive jewel-like square. He took a bite, closed his eyes, and sighed.

"Cancel everything I've ever said about candy."

"Why?"

"It was all lies. I've been living a fraudulent, Snickers-based existence."

Mikey and I traveled. We chased days with nothing but our passports and a sense of awe.

Back then, joy felt endless.

Vitals: O_2 100%. Pulse steady.

Happiness: off the charts.

~

That chocolate had a financial advisor.

My son had a soul accountant.

Something inside him was always keeping tally—of joy, of justice, of mercy.

As if he knew the world would one day charge interest on his laughter.

Chapter 13

The Mold and The Mic

Y*ou never notice the furnace until the fire touches someone you love.*

End of Summer 2018. St. Augustine

When we returned to Florida, life started folding into place, like everything we had asked for had found us.

Mikey had just been accepted into a prestigious aerospace engineering program at his new high school. His eyes lit up every time he talked about building rockets and becoming a pilot. He was fourteen and fearless. He walked with his shoulders back, like he was carrying the future and already knew how to fly it.

St. Augustine wears its history like wrinkles it's proud of; ghosts linger in doorways, smirking like they've seen it all before. Mikey's high school belonged to that world, but without the charm: it looked normal enough on orientation day with lockers that slammed too loud, vending machines that ate dollar bills without remorse and flyers curling off corkboards like autumn leaves. All standard issue for public education.

When we stepped in the aerospace classroom where Mikey would spend most of his days, I didn't know whether to cry or cough. The walls looked like someone had challenged mildew to a mural competition… and lost. Ceiling tiles sagged with the weight of black mold and forgotten budgets. If interior design had a villain, this was her masterpiece.

I wanted to light a match and run.

I tugged Larry's sleeve and gave him *the* look, the way married couples talk without words. He didn't register—the way a married man sometimes doesn't.

Ignoring the mold, carefree Mikey was off making friends, laughing, belonging like he never had before.

"This is so cool," he beamed, fist-bumping kids he hadn't seen in years, finding new ones faster than I could say "mold remediation."

He made the soccer team, then basketball. He stayed after school, laughed more than he slept, his lanky limbs carrying him across courts and fields while my bones ached just standing inside that classroom. His transcript read like ambition, his days stretched between athletics, advanced classes, and aerospace.

Weeks passed. Then months.

Every kid in that class—I mean every single one—started developing "seasonal allergies." The professor disappeared for days at a time, then weeks. Still, Mikey refused to leave.

My son was thriving in the rot.

But in me… there was a quiet rumble.

It started softly, like a minor key in a symphony—hard to place, but impossible to ignore. I felt *very* restless.

Have you ever had your soul whisper to you in a language you couldn't yet speak?

That's what my restlessness felt like. I had nowhere else to *go* with it, so one Sunday I asked the priest if he knew what I could *do* about it! "Father, is there a prayer rule? I can't stand this feeling!"

He tilted his head kindly: "There's no formula. Just speak to Him, like a child speaks to their father. Pray over it."

Hmm… I *thought* I was.

I prayed while folding laundry and stirring soup. I didn't have eloquence, just the longing to know what this feeling was all about already. And one still afternoon, with light sliding across the kitchen tiles, I whispered the prayer that would change everything:

"God, I don't know what this feeling is about, I don't know what's coming but I don't think I like it… Please draw us closer to You."

Little did I know then what closeness to God might look like. We always picture it as soft light and peaceful mornings, but sometimes—no, often—it's fire. A furnace that refines. It's everything safe being shaken loose so only the unshakable remains.

Mikey continued to play soccer, basketball, volunteer across town, always looking for a way to give back. Then he dove into Cambridge courses with the hunger only joy can drive.

He was thriving. The picture of health. The picture of promise.

The picture-perfect.

I had no idea we were already standing in the furnace I'd unconsciously asked for.

The Mic

My hybrid had become both shuttle and stage; few other kids from our neighborhood went to the same out of zone school, so every carpool was a rolling concert. We called it "Carioke." Windows down, harmonies questionable, joy unfiltered. The only rule? Nobody got out without singing.

Lila always claimed shotgun, headphones dangling around

her neck in studied indifference. Which meant, of course, she cared deeply.

"Whose playlist today?" I'd ask.

"Mine," she'd grin.

Mikey's best friend—head over heels for Lila in ways he couldn't hide—practically jumped through the ceiling.

"Great choice. Amazing taste. Literally the best—"

Mikey cut him off. "Bro, you sound like her Yelp review."

Lila laughed. He turned red. I nearly ran a stop sign.

Carioke was chaos. Blissful chaos. Cracked falsettos, spilled water bottles, teenagers howling like caffeinated wolves.

"Mikey," Lila said, flipping her braid over her shoulder, "my friend Angela likes you. Can I give her your number?"

Mikey blinked. "Uh. Yeah. I guess. Whatever." He went back to fiddling with the speaker, pretending he wasn't blushing down to his collar.

By December, we were doing off-key Christmas carols with the windows down, voices shredded by cold air and teenage conviction. Mikey laughed so hard water shot out of his nose. Golden days, glittering now only because of how fast the dark arrived.

It happened just before winter break.

Before the shadows closed in, I needed you to see the light. I had to show you the before—when joy was still whole, and Mikey was more than what was coming. Once the fire starts, you'll question everything.

But this... this was the boy before the burning.

God's joy, just before the smoke.

Chapter 14

Wrestling The Invisible Enemy

That injury lit the match. That match was the spark. The crack in the foundation. And in two discs in his neck.

Fall 2018. St. Augustine

His math teacher spotted the way he lit up for sports and invited him to join the wrestling team. Mikey committed too fast, but he wasn't built for the mat—tall, lean, Mediterranean neck made for a piano recital, not chokeholds. The mat didn't care.

We didn't know that commitment would cost him.

Mikey didn't tell me right away. He waited until the ride home, a Wednesday, I think. Still light out. His hoodie smelled like a gym floor and teenage boy.

"I think I heard something pop in my neck," he said, casually, like he was reporting a glitch in a video game.

"Like, twice. During wrestling."

My fingers tightened on the wheel.

"Pop like… 'pop and lock'?" I asked, trying to stay calm, stay jokey.

He shook his head. "No. Like… bones. When Coach demoed the reversal on me."

My mouth dried out so fast it felt like I'd swallowed sand.

"Wait! You injured your neck during wrestling practice?"

"Yeah. The coach didn't mean to hurt me; he was just showing the move on me. Neck kinda twisted weird. Then—crack, crack. Felt... wrong."

He sipped his water like it was no big deal.

I jerked the wheel and rolled us into the CVS parking lot.

"Mikey," I said slowly, turning to face him, "did you see the school nurse?"

"I mean…" He looked out the window. "It's wrestling. Stuff cracks all the time. Coach was concerned but I told him I was ok…"

"Mikey" I said, my voice low, sharp, mother-anointed. "Stuff clicks. Stuff pops. Stuff doesn't double crack in your neck like a busted glow stick."

Same smile he gave me when he had the flu and still tried to shovel the neighbor's driveway in Bosnia. "It's fine. Just sore." The way he said it made something primal in me lurch. *He was not fine.* I knew it the way animals know storms before the clouds come.

It wasn't just his neck that twisted. It was the axis of everything—his health, his future, our peace.

Something shifted out of place that day, and nothing ever aligned again.

Chapter 15

Seize the Day

Every story has two sides: The one that makes you. And the one that unmakes you. I was made by what I inherited. I was unmade the moment my child hit the floor. Lifeless. That would unmake anyone.

October 2018. St. Augustine

That night, everything was normal.

Dinner. Homework. Toothbrush left in the wrong place, again. He kept rubbing his neck and said his head felt heavy. Eyes unfocused. He looked like someone had dimmed the light inside him a few watts.

"Rest," I told him, fluffing the pillow beneath his head. "You'll feel better in the morning."

Lies. Sweet ones. Poisoned ones.

Then, just before midnight, I heard a sound I didn't recognize. Not from him. Not from *anyone.* It didn't belong to a child —or a home—or this world. It was like a wolf choking on a scream.

I ran as if my feet were made of fire. I turned the corner so fast I scraped the wall. Mikey was on the floor, eyes wild and not seeing. His body stiff, then jerking, then stiff again.

Limbs at war with themselves. Foam at the edge of his mouth. A moan so guttural I didn't recognize it as human until I realized it was coming from *my baby*.

My knees hit tile. I heard the crack of them later. Hands hovering, useless. Useless.

I kept crying his name—again and again—"Mikey! Mikey? Mikey," as if calling it could break the spell.

It didn't.

Larry burst in and dropped to the floor next to him.

"What's happening?" The words came out cracked, barely mine.

"Michael Gabriel! You answer me, right now!" I kept calling like his name was a rope I could throw into the dark and pull him back.

But he was gone.

Somewhere behind those twitching eyes, my son was gone—just for a moment, just long enough for my soul to split open. I watched as his body lost him. As the brain, the brilliant brain that could memorize *Harry Potter* spells and chess tactics and Byzantine liturgy—sputtered.

Like a candle blown out by something unseen.

Later, in a quieter moment, I realized: that was it.

The *before*.

The moment we would rewind forever. The last day we would ever describe him as *fine*.

We are living in the *after* now.

Chapter 16

Measure of a Man

The measure of a man isn't what he earns. It's what he gives away without expecting anything back.

October 2018. St. Augustine

Mikey enjoyed volunteering for various non-profits and giving his helping hands wherever he could. I remembered watching him at the Greek Festival, sweat pouring down his forehead as he hauled trash, wiped down tables, sold tickets, and finally braved the grease of the souvlaki booth. He worked all day without complaint.

The booth owner clapped him on the shoulder, grinning. "Take a break, kid. You earned it." He handed Mikey a large, foil-wrapped souvlaki as a reward—hot, heavy, and smelling like heaven. He peeled back the foil, stomach growling so loud it almost embarrassed him and was just about to take the first real bite of the day when a classmate strolled up, arm draped around his girlfriend like he was posing for a photo. Full swagger. Zero sweat.

"Yo, man," the classmate said, eyeing the food. "That looks so good."

His girlfriend made a face like she was about to faint. "Ugh, I'm starving," she said. "There's like nothing left."

Mikey's fingers tightened around the warm foil, stomach snarling louder this time.

"We waited an hour for those dumb festival games," the classmate said. "Total waste."

Mikey still wore the apron, soaked through. His volunteer T-shirt damp with sweat, a silent proof he'd spent those same hours working, not chasing tickets and thrills.

He closed his eyes for half a second, then handed the souvlaki over. "Here. Take mine."

They took it and walked away, laughing between bites.

I stood frozen, watching his hand fall to his side—empty, greasy, and still open. My mama heart twisted in my chest, pride and ache colliding in a way only mothers understand. I rushed to buy him another one. He was sitting on the curb by then, dabbing at his sweat with a napkin.

"Mikey," I said softly, handing him the food, "you didn't have to do that."

He gave a tired shrug. "They were hungry."

"So were you!" I said.

He shrugged again.

I sat beside him, said nothing. What *could* I say? Maybe he knew exactly what he'd done. Maybe he didn't care. But in that moment, I knew what kind of man he was becoming.

That night, my heart grew three sizes bigger.

And cracked a little, too.

Chapter 17

Our MESS and His MESSage

S*ome holidays carry magic. Ours carried the weight of unanswered prayers.*

December 2018. St. Augustine

The house smelled of cinnamon rolls fresh from the oven, wrapping us in a sugar-dusted hug that refused to let go. Ribbons and torn wrapping paper trailed across the floor, and Oreo strutted through the mess like he owned the season. We were curled under blankets in our well-worn Christmas pajamas, laughter bubbling between us as we watched our favorite holiday movies. Mikey pointed at the screen, half-giggling, half-appalled.

"Wait—*that's* Rudolph?" he said, eyes wide with mock horror. "He looks like a red-nosed potato!"

I chuckled. "Hey, that movie was cutting-edge back then."

He shot me a side-eye. "Cutting-edge like scissors from kindergarten?"

Then came that crinkly-eyed laugh I wanted to bottle up and keep forever. Surrounded by celebration and joy, it was easy to ignore that beneath it all, something was shifting.

Mikey kept rubbing his neck, that wrestling injury bothering him more than usual.

Then, in the blink of an eye, everything changed.

One moment we were laughing; the next, uncontrollable movements rippled through him, like a storm breaking free. A visceral, trembling moan shattered the morning like glass.

Before I could even move, Oreo was pawing at his chest, licking his forehead with desperate urgency, as if sheer love could pull him back. His fiercest protector, helpless but unwilling to let go. Just like us.

This was the second time his body was wracked with an unseen attacker. It was just as terrifying as the first.

Less terrifying than my fearful thoughts, though.

"Larry! Larry! It happened again (as if he couldn't see, as if he weren't just as scared!)! What's going on!!!

Christmas lights blinked softly in the background, peaceful and unaware, as if nothing were wrong. As if our world hadn't just cracked open beside the tree.

Christmas collapsed into ChristMESS

Gone were the glitter and gifts, the cinnamon and carols. In their place: fear. Questions.

When the seizure finally released him, I stroked his hair and cried prayers only God could decipher. The lights still twinkled. Oreo stayed pressed against his favorite human, as if his small body could shoulder what heaven already held. The gifts sat untouched beneath the tree.

Something dark and merciless had just hijacked Christmas, something we couldn't name or stop. It left behind broken pieces on the floor, the deaf silence that followed the seizure, the fragile breath I didn't realize I'd been holding until Mikey's chest finally rose again.

That morning, we didn't hold certainty or peace. But we held each other.

Was this the closeness I prayed for? Because I wasn't ready for it.

Shock and fright opened the chapter that would test our faith, our hope, and our very souls.

Chapter 18

The Pill in my Palm

I*t was just a pill, but it might as well have been a bullet. And I would spend the rest of my life wondering what life could've been if I hadn't given it to him.*

January 21, 2019. Children's Hospital

We waited three months for the first available neurology appointment. Both seizures came when Mikey's neck injury flared up. The connection was clear to us. It wasn't random or escalating, it was traceable.

But to the neurologist, it was textbook epilepsy. And the solution was textbook medication.

From the moment we sat down, I felt the quiet dismissal. The prescription was already written on his forehead before he even listened. I didn't want to argue. I just wanted answers.

The neurologist barely glanced up from the chart. "Unprovoked events you've described qualify as epilepsy. We'll start a medication called Depakote. Twice daily."

My voice was calm, but it carried the edge only mothers know how to wield. "Can we slow down a second, please?"

He looked up, blinked once, then returned to the screen. "This is the protocol."

"I'm not refusing treatment," I said carefully. "But I am asking for testing—genetic compatibility, metabolic markers, anything that could predict adverse reactions. He's never taken a drug like this before."

"That's not the routine."

"Where I come from, it is. Especially with this kind of medication."

He sighed. Loudly. "This isn't Europe."

"No," I said, eyes locked on his, "but he *is* my son."

Larry shifted beside me, his voice quiet. "We're just trying to understand all the options."

The neurologist finally looked up. Not angry, just done.

"You can either agree, or I'll have to document refusal. That affects his clearance for school sports, driver's ed. And yes, it becomes part of his file."

"You want me to say yes," I said softly, "while I still have questions."

"You're overcomplicating this," he muttered and turned back to the screen. Keys clicked.

I imagined the note in his system: *Mother resistant. Delaying care. Non-compliant.* He tore off the prescription and slid it across the desk like a parking ticket. It sat there between us, humming with consequence.

Larry looked at me. "What do you want to do?"

I stared at the page. "I want him to treat my son like he matters," I whispered.

If you've ever had your child's pain reduced to a textbook line, you know the rage that simmers beneath a polite nod. I wore a smile women wear when they're being cornered but can't afford to look angry.

"I understand. I just… I know my son. And I don't want to break something that isn't broken."

But it didn't matter.

We picked up the Depakote that night. The pill was burning a hole in my palm and sat like judgment in my hand

—small, round, indifferent to the story we were living. Mikey looked at me, wide-eyed, already knowing.

"Mom… I don't want this. This will hurt me."

How do you force a pill into your knowing child's mouth *and* crush your instincts because a white coat said to?

We prayed. We cried.

And we gave him the pill.

Seven big and long seizures over the next five days, unprovoked by neck position, sleep, or overexertion. We called the doctor and they told us to go to the ER. From there, he was admitted to the epilepsy monitoring unit.

And the verdict?

"This is the natural progression of epilepsy."

I tried to explain, to plead. "He didn't have this many before. It changed after the medication..."

"Neck injuries don't cause seizures," they said.

They didn't want to hear what made Mikey different; they wanted him to fit their mold. When I asked again about testing—just to see which meds his body *could* tolerate—they gave me a look that could wither skin. Instead of taking him off the medication that was making him worse, they added more—through IV.

I stood at the foot of his bed, arms folded so tightly my nails left crescent moons in my skin. "You're giving him more of what triggered the seizures in the first place," I said flatly.

The doctor didn't look up. "There's no evidence it caused them."

"There's no evidence it *didn't*."

He sighed, like I was exhausting. "We've seen this progression before. These clusters happen."

"No," I said. "No to *him*. Not like this. *Not until the medication*."

A nurse moved around the IV line, carefully avoiding eye contact.

The doctor turned toward me, voice low and practiced. "I understand you're concerned…" He didn't blink. "You brought him here for help," he said finally. "And this is how we help."

"But your help is hurting him."

He turned back to the monitor. The click of keys replaced any answer.

Larry's hand touched my back, gentle but firm, like a tether.

"Babe," he murmured, "this won't get him discharged any faster."

I knew he was right, but at that moment, I wasn't looking for an exit.

Within minutes: cluster of seizures. One after another.

Their response?

"We see that the high dose made no change, so… We're adding Keppra now. His seizures are not well controlled."

They shoved a new pill down his throat and left the room, their laughter trailing down the hall.

I stood there, watching the door. I was shaking but not from fear. It was fury. I was not allowed to question. I was not allowed to protect him. I *was* expected to nod while they drugged him into silence, and thank them for doing it. And in that moment, it came to me, clear as bone:

They were *not* helping him. The place built for healing had become a place that hurt him.

This wasn't medicine.

This was power.

And power, when left unquestioned, always finds a way to call itself right.

Chapter 19

Boy in Sackcloth

B*efore anything tore or shattered, there was only one thing I knew for sure: this wasn't a side effect. This was my son's soul trying to save itself, but the chart didn't have a box for that.*

July 2019. St. Augustine

Three days after introducing the new medication—Keppra, known to cause rage, though nobody bothered to warn us—we were on our way to take pictures for Mikey's new passport, a silly little errand for a boy whose biggest concern just days earlier had been running out of space in the old one.

Mikey was sitting in the back seat when everything began to shift, quietly at first, then violently. He was fully awake, and I could see in his eyes that something terrifying was happening.

Something was really, really wrong.

Without warning, he wet himself. I turned around just in time to see the fright in his face, the panic blooming beneath his skin. His hands began to tremble, and then he grabbed at his clothes—clawing, yanking, trying to tear them off like they were made of thorns. There was no logic to it, no explanation that fit. Just a boy unraveling in front of his mother, desperate to escape his own body.

His voice broke as he cried, "They are killing me! I can't take this anymore."

There was no exaggeration in those words, only clarity, and truth. What followed wasn't a fear manifesting in chaos, but a complete break from something sacred inside him. He was protesting with every cell in his body, crying out with the urgency that flesh alone cannot contain.

This was the very thing we had begged them to see, yet they dismissed it like an inconvenience.

His words unraveled into sounds, syllables breaking apart until language itself betrayed him. His limbs jerked in frantic rhythm, as if the chemicals they forced into him were rearranging his mind faster than his soul could hold his body together.

~

Then came the tearing.

It wasn't the restless tug of a boy; it felt ancient, the gesture of mourners who rip their garments when grief had nowhere else to go. He clawed at his shirt with a fury of a soul pushed to the brink of sorrow, unable to speak but letting fabric carry the prayer his body couldn't form. He ripped it to shreds, fiber by fiber, as if the cloth itself bore witness to the torment they refused to acknowledge.

I watched, frozen between heartbreak and revelation. He did not need scrolls to teach him the rituals of lament, nor prophets to model grief; his flesh understood it. His body testified.

~

But the world I had to face didn't speak of prophets or sackcloth; it spoke in numbers and vitals and charts. I drove to my office (Larry was out of town), the only place where I could measure something real, something I could name.

His blood pressure read 168 over 120. That number shouldn't exist in a teenager whose only crime was trusting us to protect him from harm we didn't know to fear.

So yes, we went back to the ER. And yes, they transferred him.

Again.

The children's hospital took him in.

Again.

The cycle repeated itself, as though the system were stuck on repeat.

Oh, the war inside me: a spirit that knew the truth against a system that wouldn't hear it; a gut that cried NO against a world that demanded YES.

They documented the visit, but not the fact that he had never been like this before the medication(s). What they did not put on the chart was the confession that Keppra caused this prophetic rage, driving him into psychosis.

But mother remembers what paper chooses to forget.

"Go home and, as per discharge papers, immediately notify your doctor..."

Blah, blah, blah.

That night, after the hospital discharged him like a glitch in the system, I went home and sat on the laundry room floor. I think I folded the same shirt for thirty minutes. It was his. It still smelled like him before everything went sideways.

I couldn't pray. I couldn't even rage.

I just sat there like a ghost, holding cotton and grief.

People ask me what the worst part is.

The seizures? No.

The meds? No.

The marriage? Not even close.

It's the waiting.

Waiting for the system to wake up.

Waiting for one doctor to actually look at Mikey and see what I see.

Waiting for answers that never seem to come when you need them.

I've learned that waiting can break you in slow motion.

You don't realize it's happening until you look back and see how much of yourself you left in hospital rooms and parking lots and late-night phone calls.

I looked at my son and barely recognized him.

I survived genocide, but *nothing* prepared me for navigating American health care.

As for faith…

I used to think it meant understanding what God was doing. Now I think it's what you hang onto when you understand nothing at all.

Child-me used to picture God calm and clean, high on a mountaintop, beard flowing like some celestial therapist. Keeping score, untouched by pain.

Now?

Now, I picture Him slumped next to me in a hospital chair. Silent. Blood on His robe.

Like He got bit by the snake, too.

Chapter 20

The Snakes Among Us

I *used to think you could spot the dangerous ones. Then came the snakes that smiled first.*

Summer, 2009. Florida

I should have known silence meant trouble.

It was one of those thick, blistering Florida afternoons. Mikey was five, playing in the yard. I was half-reading by the window when I saw him stretched out flat on the curb, arm extended, motionless.

For a second, I couldn't breathe thinking he'd collapsed. I bolted outside, barefoot on scorched pavement, panic already climbing my spine. My lungs burned before my feet did. I reached for him, but before my fingers brushed his skin, that curly head popped up. Calm eyes blinked at me, sun spilling across his face.

"What's wrong, Mama? Are you okay?"

He wasn't the one in danger—at least not in his mind. I collapsed onto the curb beside him, half-crying, half-laughing from the whiplash of terror. He pointed at a baby snake, its thin, colorful body coiled like a question mark. I was two seconds from cardiac arrest. I yanked him back like that little thing had fangs—for all I knew, it did.

"She's not mean," he said matter-of-factly. "She's just waiting."

He didn't know how much truth lived in that sentence.

I gave him the eye.

"She's lost," he said. "I felt sorry for her, so I petted her."

"Mikey, baby," I said, "where there's a baby snake, there's probably a mama snake. And she's not gonna want to talk about her feelings. Not in Florida."

He sighed like I just didn't get it, hands still sticky from sympathy.

Where I saw danger, he saw vulnerability. Where I saw a threat, he saw a soul needing kindness.

I'd think of that day —

Maybe he already knew what it meant to reach out, even if it meant getting bit.

We thought it was a baby snake.

We thought if we reached out with kindness, with trust, maybe it would recognize that we weren't the enemy.

But snakes don't change their nature.

They strike.

And then they slither back into the system that protects them.

Chapter 21

He Seized. They Celebrated.

The sky lit up like joy had no consequences. While America celebrated its freedom, our son was learning what it meant to have none.

July 4, 2019. Children's Hospital

Eight grand mal seizures on the way home from the ER. Twelve by the time we hit the driveway.

We couldn't stop it. We had nothing to give.

We were helpless, reduced to witnesses.

We called 911. Again. Another ambulance. Another small-town ER. Another urgent transfer back to the children's hospital that had just pushed us out the door. The ER doctor looked at me like I was holding a live wire.

"They never should've stopped a high dose like that. Did they give you a bridge med?"

A bridge—what?

Children's Hospital, we need to talk!

They stopped the Keppra without a taper, and without offering any plan to transition off the medication safely. It was handled as though a high-dose anticonvulsant could be removed from a child's system without consequence, as if the body would not notice, as if nothing would backfire. There was no substitute, no slow reduction, no conversation about what might follow. We learned the hard way:

You stop Keppra cold?

The seizures come hot.

Breakthroughs. Clustered. Violent. One after another.

And they can *kill*.

By the time that lesson lit my son's body like a fuse, it was too late.

There's no manual for this kind of heartbreak.

It was the Fourth of July weekend. Fireworks burst outside the hospital window, the night sky glittering with celebration. Inside, my son's brain misfired like a firework gone wrong—sparks without rhythm, explosions without beauty. Larry and I held hands so tight it hurt.

The world was celebrating.

My son was seizing.

The attendings were MIA. The residents said they were "understaffed." Nurses whispered, "There's nothing we can do without orders."

Phones rang into silence as he seized all night, from the late hours to the thin ones.

The snake coiled, and the venom kept spreading.

Twelve more seizures by 6 a.m. I counted. I watched. I feared what it was doing to his beautiful brain.

"Get somebody already! I don't care if it's a holiday. I don't care if you're short-staffed. A child should not be the one to pay the price for their celebrations."

Finally, someone called a rapid response. And they were

rapid—warriors in scrubs who moved like fire through smoke, pulling him back from the edge. A resident finally woke up, walked in *after* they stabilized him. She spoke to him like her presence could undo her silence.

I told her she was twelve seizures too late. I told her to step away from my son.

She looked at me like my fury was the problem, but the rapid team took our side.

"You need a patient advocate," they said.

A patient—what?

Nobody had ever spoken those words to me. Or explained what our rights were.

What MIKEY'S rights were!

Before this discharge, I filed a complaint. Days later, a letter arrived from the hospital director.

"Apologies on behalf of the residents."

But no apology could send us back in time, before the Keppra was stopped, and before what those twelve seizures did to his brain. Before I screamed into a void for help.

It didn't ease his suffering, and it couldn't soften mine.

Chapter 22

I Died 1,000 Times

D*ying isn't what kills you. It's the moment you realize you can't stop it.*

July 2019. 1,000 seizures later

I died a thousand times that Fourth of July. Quietly, in ways no one could see.

Mikey barely made it through the night. His eyelids fluttered open, shock and disappointment settling as he recognized where he was.

"Can we *please* go home?"

He already knew what this place did to him.

"How much longer?" he asked. "How many more of these, Mama?"

I wished I had an answer. I still don't.

At only fifteen, his life had shifted from becoming to enduring. It began to pull inward, like a house shutting its windows one by one.

I thought I had already walked through every dark valley a mother could: misdiagnoses, endless waiting rooms, the polite dismissal from doctors who thought I was imagining things. Who thought he was.

But this was different.

This was a slow goodbye, watching the boy who once ran barefoot through the yard with his arms wide like wings turn into someone I couldn't reach. A body I could hold, but not save.

"Let's wait," they said in measured tones, as if this were just a chapter in a book that promised a tidy ending.

As if my son had time.

They discharged us.

Larry drove us home in silence, knuckles white against the wheel.

I sat in the back seat with Mikey. His head against my chest, every breath uneven but stubborn. I wrapped my arms around him, rocking gently with the rhythm of the road. My shirt was damp where his cheek lay, but I didn't move.

If I moved, he might wake up.

If he woke up, he might seize again.

Larry glanced in the rearview mirror, our eyes meeting for just a heartbeat. The silence between us said everything: fear, exhaustion, and a love stretched to its breaking point—but still holding.

Streetlights flickered across his face, and I held him the way I did when he was a baby and couldn't sleep unless he felt my heart beating.

I held him like the night might take him if I let go.

Chapter 23

The Day the Music Broke

You always think there will be more time. More mornings. More music. One more concert. Until your child falls out of the song.

December 13, 2019. St. Augustine

That Friday morning felt like any other.

The coffee was brewing. The December light came in soft and gold. Mikey walked into the kitchen, grinning like he owned the world.

"Good morning, my Mustache Boy!"

He grinned, half amused, half insulted.

"Mom, I'll be sixteen soon. It's not Mustache Boy. I'm a Mustache MAN."

I rolled my eyes. "*Whatever.*"

Years of shared mornings, of easy banter and inside jokes, wrapped in that moment like a bow.

It was the Friday before the concert. The date had been sitting on the calendar for weeks, quietly claiming the day. Mikey's youth chorus and my adult choir would sing together for the first time, our voices rising under the same roof, offered to the same light. The joy of it had arrived early, certain of itself, but it didn't last.

I was halfway through my mascara when I heard it.

Another one.

I ran. Heart in my throat, adrenaline in my legs. I found Mikey on the floor, Larry crouched beneath him, having caught our son's fall with his own body. I dropped to my knees and rolled Mikey onto his side. I counted the seconds because they were still moving. I prayed because nothing else would.

The ambulance was responsive.

Mikey was not.

A few hours later, he was discharged from the ER. We had been trying to schedule a neurologist since the first ambulance ride in October. Nothing until January.

The concert was still scheduled. Mikey, despite everything that had just occurred, insisted on going.

"I'm singing to God, Mom. And it's in God's house," he said, steady as a storm anchor. "I'm going."

I didn't argue. How could I? When faith speaks that boldly, even fear listens.

We stood on opposite ends of the stage—me far right, Mikey far left. Larry was in the front pew, eyes fixed on our Miracle Child.

Mikey's group sang, but the only voice I could hear was *his*–clear and strong, filling the church and every heart in it. His face was lit from within, brighter than the stage lights.

When their song finished, they stepped off the risers to line up. Then, from across the stage, I saw it.

No sound.

Friends from the chorus caught him mid-collapse. Larry reached him in seconds, gathering him into his arms like a broken-winged bird. Most of the audience never noticed; the music never stopped.

But I did.

I stood there, frozen, unable to move from where I was standing. Voice trembling. Eyes birthing tears I couldn't wipe.

Still singing, because the music demanded it. Because Mikey would have wanted it.

Because I didn't know what else to do.

And then came that sweeping movement from Handel's *Messiah*—

"And the glory of the Lord… shall be revealed."

I had sung it a hundred times before, but that night it sang to *me*. It gathered me the way Larry gathered Mikey, arms closing around a body while the soul tried to lift itself, desperate to outrun the pain.

Love held him.

The melody held me—each still believing in glory.

Don't Let the Devil Win

The next morning, Sunday.

He lay beneath the weighted blanket, pale and spent, barely able to form words. The second concert never entered my mind. Standing onstage, singing to an audience while he stayed behind, felt impossible. It felt wrong.

Mikey looked at me with fire in his eyes, fierce and calm all at once.

"Mom," he said. "I want you to go."

Tears welled before I could argue. "I can't leave you. I—"

"Go. Sing for both of us," he said without flinching. "The devil would love that, for you to give up. Don't let him."

My child, in the weakest body he had ever known, still insisting I go.

I stood because he asked me to.

My legs didn't want to carry me. Mikey made them march.

The second concert was in the grand Basilica Cathedral downtown. Marble floors, arched ceilings, acoustics that seemed to bend sound into prayer. I stood on the stage, throat raw from crying, heart torn open. And then, right across the stage and from where I was standing, I saw the rustic sign on the wall that said:

"There is no misery that could be a match for my mercy."

My misery blinked up at that–standing in heels, mascara smeared, voice shaking—and somehow believed it.

All the pain that couldn't speak for itself began to sing.

For Mikey.

For mothers sobbing in emergency rooms. Children trapped in broken bodies.

The fragile thread of hope hadn't snapped yet. And in that holy, trembling moment, I still believed that healing was possible.

I whispered, "Not today, devil."

Hand That Squeezed Back

That night, I couldn't sleep.

I stood in the kitchen, eyes lifted toward the ceiling like it was the whole sky, and I begged out loud: "God… I'm asking for Mikey's miraculous healing. Before Christmas would be great. Now would be better. Please. Heal my baby."

Then I cried to Her… I whispered, my voice trembling. "You know the sword that pierces a mother's soul. Hold Mikey in your hands: hands that once carried joy and sorrow. Ask your Son to heal mine. I'm begging You, one pierced-soul mother to another."

I walked down the hallway and peeked into Mikey's room. I slid onto the bed beside him, careful not to shift the mattress. My body throbbed with exhaustion, but my mind refused to shut down. I was afraid to close my eyes. Afraid of what I might wake up to… or not.

I kept praying with silent tears slipping into the pillow. He rolled to the side, saw me smile at him and muttered: "This place hums like a spaceship. If I start floating, don't panic."

If it weren't so sad I would've laughed.

Outside, Christmas lights blinked in other people's windows. Joy in every home but ours. I closed my eyes for just a second. Reached for Mikey's hand.

And then—

He squeezed back.

Chapter 24

Sixteen and Seen

M*ost kids get a car on their sixteenth birthday. Mikey got a room full of people who weren't sure he'd make it to seventeen.*

February 2020. St. Augustine

By the time his sixteenth birthday arrived, life had already changed its rules. Seizures quietly rearranged everything, teaching us to measure time not in years, but in moments. We knew the care meant to help him wasn't leading him toward healing. So we did what we could do, right away: we surrounded him with joy.

This couldn't be just a birthday.

It had to be a Sweet Sixteen caked with new hope.

A friend who managed an oceanside restaurant gave us the spacious top floor for Mikey's party. Word spread like fire through our town. When the day came, the rooftop filled beyond expectation. More than three hundred people gathered, smiling, laughing, quietly insisting that healing was still possible.

It wasn't just a party. It was a parade of every life Mikey had touched.

Some Candles Don't Go Out

When his Sweet Sixteen finally came, half the town showed up for him. Our church family came. His teachers, from kindergarten through high school, came. Boy Scouts. Soccer and basketball teammates. Healers. Artists. Even an Army chaplain who sang Frank Sinatra better than Sinatra himself.

For one night, the city became the older brother he had once wished for.

~

And then came the part only teenagers can deliver. Drama. In stereo.

Somewhere in the crowd, Nadia arrived with her parents. Mikey's eyes lit up just enough for me to notice. Apparently, I wasn't the only one paying attention. Angela, the girl from high school who had been texting him *Hi :)* on an endless loop like it was a full-time job, showed up too.

Mikey, sweet and unfailingly polite, smiled when the moment called for it.

But his eyes kept finding Nadia.

Nadia caught on. She leaned in closer, amused. Angela hovered nearby.

"Hi, Mikey!"

He smiled. Courtesy over chemistry.

Then he looked back at Nadia.

She grinned. "So," she said, nodding toward Angela, "is that your girlfriend? She's chasing you like you're free pizza."

Right on cue. "Hi, Mikey!"

Nadia didn't miss a beat. "With extra cheese."

Mikey turned redder than the frosting on his cake. From somewhere behind him, one of his friends muttered, "Bro. You're doomed."

I found myself watching more than laughing. Only a few months earlier, we weren't sure he would even make it this far.

Larry's hand found mine. We stood there, fingers tightly intertwined, watching our son be sixteen; standing tall and confident beneath the fairy lights, girls competing for his attention like he was the last cupcake on the table. The unwilling star of his own sitcom.

Just behind him, my father quietly stepped half a pace closer. Not enough to be noticed, but just enough to reach him if gravity had other plans.

When Mikey finally blew out the candles, the smoke curled into the night. He closed his eyes for a beat, then looked out at the crowd and smiled, as if the wish had already been granted.

The surprises didn't stop on the rooftop.

When we pulled back into the driveway that night, the front yard was transformed. His high school friends had covered it with balloons, streamers, and a massive *Happy sixteenth, Mikey!* sign big enough to stop traffic. It looked like joy itself had spilled across our lawn and refused to clean up after itself.

Mikey's phone buzzed nonstop. Message after message lit up the screen, most of them merciless in the best way.

"Extra cheese!"

"Bro, you're never living that down."

And just when I thought my heart couldn't hold any more, the school choir—away on their trip in New York City—sent their voices home.

On the big screen, from the middle of Times Square, they sent us a video: a chorus of teenagers singing *Happy Birthday* over the city noise and neon lights.

I don't think I've ever seen Mikey look so stunned. So honored. So lit from the inside. A boy who had given and given, suddenly flooded with love rushing back to him in every color, every chord.

That, I realized, was a miracle of its own.

He stood there, phone buzzing with teases and emojis, eyes searching the skyline like he was waiting for the next miracle.

I didn't stop him.

Let the night be long. Let the joy last. After everything, he deserved to stand still in the light.

Some candles just don't go out.

Chapter 25

The Longest Hour

B*efore the ambulance came, before the sirens screamed, before the sun even came up—my son's heart stopped beating under my hands.*

March 1, 2020. 5:00 a.m.

That haunted hour when even the angels seem to hold their breath. The scream that pierced the silence wasn't his first, but it was the one I will never unhear. It was the sound of a soul splitting at the seam.

My son's body arched against the mattress like a violin string pulled too tight. No warning, no mercy. He seized, then seized again. Rescue meds—nothing.

Another seizure, 30 minutes later.

Then five-minute gaps.

Then 30 seconds.

Then—none.

His face—the soft one I kissed at bedtime—turned the color of the sky before a tornado. No rise in his chest. No spark in his eyes. Just stillness. And silence. For one breathless moment, the earth seemed to stop moving with me, as if even time refused to witness this.

I had just witnessed the death of my child.

I let out a raw, earth-shaking wail—anguish only a mother's soul in pieces can summon. I screamed for God. Begged. Bargained. Demanded heaven's attention, praying with fists clenched.

His teenage frame lay limp beneath my hands as I breathed into him, pressed on his ribs, counted beats with shaking hands.

CPR, just as I'd been taught—pumping to the rhythm of *"Stayin' Alive."* But the lyrics made me cry. Hands of time tripped and fell into a memory of his wiggly little butt dancing in the school gym to that very song.

"Stayin' alive, stayin' alive…"

Ah, my broken heart, *MIKEY—STAY ALIVE! YOU HEAR ME?!!!*

Larry called 911. The dispatcher guided us again through compressions, but we didn't need a script.

We needed a miracle.

~

This is SUDEP. Sudden Unexpected Death in Epilepsy.

A monster that sleeps under our beds and wakes hungry. And we were wide awake.

I was still performing CPR, refusing to stop even when his heart did.

The ambulance came—blue lights, red fear. They loaded him up and closed the doors, refusing to let me ride with him. I screamed and fell to my knees as they drove him away, leaving me on the curb with my hands shaking and my heart outside my body.

I had no breath left to call after him.

Inside that screaming box on wheels, the seizures raged on. No relief.

Just straps, sirens and terror. We followed behind, headlights off, both of us numb.

Behind the Curtains

At the hospital, they closed the curtain and wouldn't let me near him. From the other side I watched the shadows of his body seize again and again. I stood there, useless.

He convulsed while doctors discussed options, too busy to turn him to his side so he wouldn't drown in his own saliva. No oxygen after seizures, no urgency. He choked, and pneumonia moved in like a squatter.

I pleaded with my eyes. Then came the words that shattered whatever resolve I had left:

"We're initiating an emergency transfer to NE Florida Critical Neuro Care."

Death hovered, just a breath away. I believe that was the only reason they let me ride with him.

I held his hand and watched: his chest—too still; his lips—too pale.

The machine beeped behind us like it was losing patience.

The paramedics moved quickly, but the air was heavy with a message:

Don't get your hopes up.

Was It My Singing?

The sirens screamed, meant to warn, to bring help, to say life was still worth the fight. To me it was the soundtrack of loss, and I did the only thing I could think to do: I sang.

"You are my sunshine, my only sunshine…" The sirens were too loud, and I needed him to hear *me*, not the world falling apart.

"You make me happy when skies are gray…" His hand was still, eyes closed. I leaned closer, barely able to breathe, barely able to keep going. Clutching his hand like a lifeline, I let myself fall into memory—the only place where he still laughed.

He was three years old, curly-haired, eyes full of mischief, like he knew something the world had forgotten. We were on the porch swing, bare feet dangling, the warmth of evening wrapped around us like a soft blanket.

I was singing the same song: *"You'll never know dear, how much I love you…"*

But before I could finish, he tugged my hand, looked up, and grinned like he had just outsmarted the universe. "No, *Y-O-U are MY* sunshine."

God, how I missed that boy.

Now he was slipping between worlds, and I could only hold on to the part of him that was still here.

Back in the ambulance, I started the last line. "Please don't take my sunshine away… "

Please, God. Don't take my sunshine away.

Then, a twitch. Just a small one, but real. His fingers moved. Normally, we would've joked and I'd ask, "Was it my singing?!"

That tiny flicker of life wasn't much, yet it was everything to *me*. Hope, trembling in the shape of a finger.

I grabbed his hand tighter and kept singing.

I held on to him because I didn't know how to live in a world where he wasn't.

Chapter 26

Fools and Horses

T*he morning tried to kill him. The afternoon tried to finish the job.*

March 1, 2020. NE Florida

We arrived at Riverbend Medical Center, NE Florida just before 1:00 p.m. They rushed him inside without a word.

A new team. New wires. New questions.

Same nightmare.

I followed them through the doors like a ghost; no one stopped me this time. I think even they could see I was the only thing tethering him to this world. Machines surrounded his body, now even paler than before. He looked like a boy who had fought a hundred battles in a single morning.

Because he had.

Nobody looked me in the eye. The doctors began speaking quickly—terms and plans, doses and options.

One of them said *"Intubate."* Another "Prolonged Q wave."

My body turned to ice. Then came the suggestion I couldn't stomach:

"We'd like to try a new anti-epileptic medication..."

That's when something snapped in me.

"No!"

They all turned, startled.

"I said—no. He's been on the wrong medications for fifteen months now. You don't get to experiment on my son anymore."

I could feel the nausea rising, but I stood my ground.

This wasn't medicine, it was a roulette, and my son was the one spinning.

Pharmaceutical Fiasco

March 4, 2020. NE Florida *ICU*

1,252 seizures logged

While the rest of the world whispered about Corona, we faced neurological chaos that no mask could hide. Our world had already collapsed behind the closed doors of yet another emergency room.

Without telling us, they loaded him with a new cocktail of anti-seizure drugs and within minutes, angry red welts appeared across his torso. Mikey stared down at his chest and muttered,

"Guess I'm starring in the side-effects commercial now."

"Probably nothing," the attending physician said.

But I'd been here before. I took photos and emailed them to his "Pinky Nail" neurologist in NE Florida. His reply was direct:

"Do *not* add that fourth medication (Dilantin). The rash is an allergic reaction. The cluster of seizures Tuesday night was likely a withdrawal from the overload we gave him last week. We are sending a referral to Ohio hospital for surgical evaluation."

My voice caught in my throat. Each pill felt like a stone pressed onto his chest, and each dismissal laid another onto mine.

How is this still happening?

This pattern is too familiar: a rush of medications meant to help, followed by the fallout when they're abruptly stopped. Sometimes it's a holiday, sometimes a weekend.

Always a reason.

Never a solution.

Then they send us home like it's under control. But *they* don't go home with a child who might not wake up.

High Horse and a Humble Donkey

What's the difference between a neurologist and God? God doesn't think He's a doctor.

March 2, 2020. St. Augustine

I don't know who first scrawled that bitter joke, but I know the weight behind the punchline. The sting of being overlooked, misdiagnosed, and handed the broom to sweep up the fallout? That part I know all too well.

I kept thinking about them, those gods in white coats. They descend like royalty from Mount Olympus, make their grand rounds, clipboards in hand, eyes scanning charts but never really *seeing* the child in the bed or the mother breaking beside him. They came when it suited them, left when it didn't. Then they'd ride off into the sunset, leaving families like ours to pick up the pieces.

It was 2 a.m. I glanced at Mikey and found him staring at me, eyes blank. In this house, silence didn't mean rest, it meant risk:

Is he still breathing? Did we miss it? Will we wake to a stillness we can't undo?

What if he slipped away in the night and I slept… How would I *ever* forgive myself for closing my eyes? How would I *ever* be able to find peace again?

Beside us, Larry snored—steady, oblivious. At least one of us was resting, gaining strength to carry what little hope was left. I kept casting my worries to God, but they tumbled back down like stones, landing heavy. And when you're sleep-deprived, defeat starts to feel like gravity.

I know my joke was harsh. But it's hard to trust them after *four* pharmaceutical fiascos that almost claimed his life.

So, I lay my trust at the feet of the One who rode into Jerusalem on a humble donkey, not a high horse.

Let him sleep tonight. And while You're at it…maybe quiet Larry's snoring? Amen?

A Candle for My Mustache Man

March 4, 2020.

Sleep used to visit. Now it keeps slipping further away with every restless night and in its absence, grief rummages through the house taking what it wants: a moment, a memory. Tomorrows.

Some days, the fight is nothing more than lifting a ribcage. I put on smile number nineteen and went to work.

A sweet patient made me cry, her kindness slicing through the fog like light under a closed door.

Dr. Smith," she said softly, "I was on vacation in Brazil when I read your last post. I'm not religious but I went to a church and lit a candle for your Mustache Man. For his healing."

I gently thanked her, keeping the tearless façade intact.

~

Right after his sixteenth birthday, Mikey wrote this thank-you letter. At the time, I tucked it away as a sweet memory. Today, it reads like something more—a young man's light, almost prophetic in its timing.

I may not know all of you that have supported me through this struggle or those that showed up at my birthday party, but I do know one thing. It's that you care about me and your prayers and donations have given me more strength and happiness than I had no idea was humanly possible. You took time to pray, to write letters, to visit and support me, and I can't even begin to express my gratitude! This young Mustache Man is overflowing with affection!

Even though I appreciate all of this, I appreciate the loving most of all. It has cheered me up when times were rough and taught me some incredible lessons, and the least I can do is tell you what your kindness taught me. Negativity does nothing! I couldn't have become a better, wiser, and happier Mustache Man without all of you, and I just want to help you live a happier life as well.

I've made new and lasting friendships and received treasures more valuable than gold or any precious metal. People have helped me heal with laughter. People have helped me heal with generosity, with unexpected visits, by "hanging out" with me. I could go on and on for ages, but I just have one thing to say really, and it's that all the money in the world is nowhere near as valuable as YOUR loving spirits.

Your actions should be the definition of love, and I hope that the incredible deeds you did to help my life also help your lives, and that you all can enjoy your lives in peace, love, joy, and happiness.

I love each and every one of you.

—Mikey Smith

A.K.A. The Mustache Man

I poured words into him when he was young, and at sixteen, he poured them back into the world. His thank-you letter was more than gratitude—it was testimony.

A songbird's song, even from inside the cage.

Part III: Prisoners of Hope

For a long time, we believed healing was something you moved toward.
Slowly, imperfectly, but forward all the same.

But there came a point when the forward motion stopped.
Hope stopped being answered in the way we had come to expect.
This is the moment the story stopped being about healing and became about enduring the wounds that healing couldn't close.

Chapter 27

The Doctor Who Looked Twice

Hope had become dangerous. Fragile enough to shatter at the faintest touch, and just as easily weaponized by those who meant well but never stayed long enough to feel the cost.

March 5, 2020.

By the time we stepped into the exam room of the doctor who would change everything, Mikey had already endured six hospital admissions, nine failed medications, and more than a thousand seizures. Each one had taken something from him.

Each one collected its toll from our faith.

We had scheduled this appointment weeks earlier, back when time still felt negotiable. Dr. Suzanne had been just another name on a dwindling list—a Hail Mary cast into a sky already dark with worry. Back then, "getting answers" had seemed like something you could pencil between soccer practice and school pick-ups.

Before survival became something measured with a stopwatch.

Dr. Z didn't sweep into the room with a white coat or a clipboard, the props of authority. There was no exaggerated smile, no singsong voice designed to coax compliance. She entered quietly, carrying herself like someone who understood storms and did not fear them. And when her eyes settled on Mikey, she *saw* him.

She pulled up a chair and smiled. "So, what do you like being called?"

"Mikey," he said. Then, with a faint smirk, "A.K.A. the Mustache Man."

"Oh! Royalty." She gave a tiny bow. "Nice to meet you, Mustache Man."

He answered with a soft nod, like he was granting permission.

And so, we began.

Her questions came like a net cast wide, pulling in details no neurologist had ever thought to ask. Not only symptoms and medications, but pets, travel, sleep patterns, vaccine dates, tick bites from his Boy Scout years, forgotten exposures, and random events we had dismissed long ago.

When she asked about a kitten, I almost brushed it aside.

The memory had softened with time, pushed to the edges by everything that happened after, until her question brought it back into focus. I told her how he had tried to help the sickly kitten, how the scratch bled, how we cleaned it and moved on because it never seemed like something that would matter later.

Mikey shifted in his seat, eyes dropping to the scar from the scratch.

"She was scared," I said. "That's why she scratched, it panicked."

He nodded. "…and so did you."

I rolled my eyes, and for a second, we almost smiled in that exam room.

Then *I* nodded, not at the scratch now, but at the tenderness in him that never changed.

Dr. Z's eyes sharpened, her attention narrowing to a point, and she leaned in the slightest bit. "Thank you for telling me that," she said, low and deliberate.

I blinked. "Why?"

"There's something I want to test him for. It's rare," she replied, careful with every word, "but possible."

I waited, my heart thudding. She exhaled, then gave the name as if unveiling a hidden truth.

"Cat Scratch Disease."

A hollow laugh slipped out before I could stop it. "That's an actual thing?"

Her lips curved into the faintest smile. "Yes. And if he has it… it could explain a lot."

Mikey frowned, shifting in his chair. "From a cat scratch? That sounds… ridiculous."

"It does," she admitted, her voice steady, "but Bartonella—the bacteria behind Cat Scratch Disease—can do more than most people realize. In rare cases, it affects the nervous system and can cause seizures. Even fatal status epilepticus."

"So, you're saying all this"—he waved his hand, as if the seizures, the medications, the hospital stays could be swept into a single gesture—"might have come from a *kitten*?"

Her gaze didn't waver. "I'm saying it's possible. Not certain, but possible."

He looked at me, then back at her, the hardness in his eyes softening.

"And if it is?"

"Then," she said, calm as stone, "we'll finally have a place to start."

I leaned forward. "But why would it wait for two years to get angry?"

Her answer came without hesitation, as though she had already traced the storm to its source. "Because his neck injury created the Perfect Storm, compromising his blood-brain barrier. Opportunistic infections lie in wait for moments like that. For Mikey, it wasn't just the cat. It was the black mold in his classroom, the trauma to his neck, and then the medications his body couldn't handle. By the time you tested, you already knew he was allergic to the very first drug they forced on him… *Depakote*."

The words settled over me with a weight that felt strangely like relief. What she said didn't sound dismissive or far-fetched.

It made sense.

Without theatrics or false urgency, she explained the next steps: a specialized test, a follow-up in two weeks, and—if confirmed—admission to a hospital still open despite COVID restrictions, where neurology and infectious disease could work together. She handed us a kit, the instructions clear and firm in her voice.

For the first time in months, we left a doctor's office with more than prescription slips. We left with something infinitely rarer: the sense that someone had actually listened without ever making us feel that we were imagining things or exaggerating.

We weren't crazy.

In the car, Larry held the test kit in his hands, as though it were both a time bomb and a life raft.

And then we waited.

Chapter 28

Bags Full of Prayers

You don't pack for a miracle. But you keep expecting one anyway.

March 17-21, 2020. Admission to Ohio Hospital

In the waiting for the Lyme and Bartonella test results, life continued. Referral for the Ohio testing finally came through.

Could this be the answer?

I opened the suitcase and realized half of Mikey's socks were missing again. It didn't matter how many pairs I bought, they kept disappearing like they were participating in some private migration. I checked under the bed out of habit, and there it was: Oreo curled on Mikey's blanket, a few stolen socks tucked under his paw like it belonged to him.

"He's been doing that since Mikey left last time," Larry said from behind me, sorting the chargers. "Taking something that smells like him."

I gently pulled the socks free, and Oreo lifted his head, eyes following it like I'd taken something sacred.

"It's okay," I whispered, placing the blanket back beside him. "You can keep that one."

Larry held up a knot of tangled cords. "Pack or purge?"

"Pack," I said. "We lose everything else anyway."

He nodded, and we went back to the quiet work of folding and gathering, the room settling into that strange stillness that always came before a trip we didn't want to take.

We packed slowly, deliberately. Every zipper sealed a whispered prayer; every bag held a fragile heartbeat of faith. Beneath it all was a crushing ache. We held our breath and prayed that this (tenth) hospital stay in Ohio would finally be the miracle Mikey needed.

This time, we told ourselves. *This time will be different.*

We cooked dinner together, music jamming, Mikey dancing—his rhythm a little off, but his joy, perfect. We carried full bellies to our cuddle places and just enjoyed each other, each lost in our own thoughts.

While Larry and Mikey debated which comedy to watch that night, I looked out the window and saw the neighbor's boy, Mikey's age, teaching his little brother to shoot a basketball.

I watched longer than I meant to.

The ball arced, kissed the rim, fell. He whooped; the little one echoed him.

I smiled until my throat tightened, until the smile slowly slipped away.

Mikey had been so good once. Sweat at his hairline, the clock coughing its final second, the net snapping when he hit the winner. Alive. Bright with promise.

Tomorrow, we would enter a different court.

When the Wings Are Wet

March 2020. Ohio Hospital

The Ohio air cut through me, but the ache inside my heart cut deeper. Waiting has its own weather: you stand in the rain without shelter while tests fall like cold drops on fragile wings.

It's my birthday, another one in hospital.

Mikey lay beside me, spent; his body a landscape of unseen battles, his spirit a small fire cupped against the wind. Hours stretched, each one strung taut between hope and fear.

I whispered Isaiah as both prayer and plea: *Those who wait…will soar.* Right now, our wings are wet. Even so, soaked feathers carry their own promise: the sun comes back; the wind remembers us.

The days blurred into scans and monitors, and voices so measured they never reached the heart.

"Mom," he whispered, "what's wrong with me? Why can't they fix it?"

I climbed into his bed and wrapped myself around him, breathing him in.

"You are *not* broken, baby. You are becoming."

I sat in an uncomfortable hospital chair with a blanket pulled around my shoulders, still wearing yesterday's clothes, holding my breath as if any slight movement might stir the storm.

And then—the light.

A thin amber thread slipped across the floor first, quiet as a question. Minutes later it widened, orange and gold softening the sterile white and settling over Mikey's face like a benediction.

A thought broke through the fog: We made it. Another night over. Another day begun. It shouldn't feel like a miracle, but it did.

If you've ever lived hour by hour, breath by borrowed breath—when answers lag and fear arrives on schedule at dusk—the sunrise becomes everything. Proof the world is still turning. After the chaos and the silence and the pleading and the breaking—the sun still rises.

Mikey's sun-kissed eyes opened slowly, taking in this

moment, this overlooked small sunrise many take for granted, and asked:

"Mama… do you still believe in miracles?"

My breath caught. I nodded through tears. "Yes, baby. More than ever."

He gave me a weak smile—half spark, half lifeline—and I held it like a relic.

Wars had taught me to keep my chin up, sing in the hardest hours, and laugh when the heart bled. Today, the lesson returned: laughter *is* medicine. Different basement, though. His smile, for the first time in what felt like forever, no longer felt heavy. It felt like something returning.

The wings were still wet—but the light was here, and the wind was learning our names.

Discharged Into Chaos

Outside our window, COVID tightened its grip. Inside, the room did the same.

We were no longer just a family in crisis; we were part of a crisis no one could outrun. Beds were scarce, hallways filled and the hospital was bracing for the impact.

By noon the team swarmed in—charts and scans like battle plans—language ricocheting off tile: sharp, fast, too much.

The truth finally surfaced, soft and terrible: "We don't see anything structurally wrong with his brain. We can try more medications, but right now… we can't figure it out."

We expected answers but were given discharge papers instead.

So, we packed.

Mikey was quieter than ever; the curve of the oxygen cannula still pressed into his cheeks. We left behind IV poles and monitor beeps, the nurses I'd come to trust. No walls to shield him, no numbers to steady me. No call button when the floor tilted.

We left through corridors that now looked like war zones. Carts rushed past, staff in hazmat suits shouted orders, visitors were banned.

The elevator closed and the silence settled around us like a truth I was not ready to name.

We were being sent into a world as fragile as the mustached child I held beside me.

A fragile miracle with no map home.

All we had were another set of discharge papers and more *We Don't Knows*.

I folded the papers.

I took his hand, and we stepped into the fire not knowing how close the flames already were.

Chapter 29

Diagnosis That Moves

W*e finally received what we had been waiting for: a diagnosis. But knowing what something is does not mean knowing how to live with it.*

March, 2020.

Twelve days later, on a Thursday morning just after ten, the call arrived. The moment I saw the number, my heart recognized the significance of the moment before my mind did. Something in me already sensed that whatever came next would alter the path we were on. When I finally answered, that feeling proved correct.

The call from Dr. Z had given us what we were desperate for—an answer, a name, a proper diagnosis and a way forward. Once the words were spoken, the reality of what needed to happen next arrived immediately. It was time to pack, prepare and move.

Packing Hope

Sixteen is for learner's permits, texting friends late into the night, first jobs, and flirting with the edges of freedom.

Mikey was packing for another hospital stay.

His backpack should have carried the restless clutter of teenage years, like hoodies and headphones, a phone charger tangled with dreams of future. Instead, it carried something else entirely.

Into his backpack went The Book Thief, its pages dog-eared from weeks of interrupted reading. He slid in his Cambridge binder as if it were a passport, a piece of himself he refused to surrender to illness.

"You packing half the library?" I asked.

He shrugged. "Well, if I pass out again, I want to come back to something worth reading."

I raised a brow. "What about clothes?"

He smirked. "Books take priority. Clothes are optional."

We couldn't help but laugh. Then he zipped the bag and the room felt heavy again.

By March 2020, he was placed in a hospital-homebound program, studying from our kitchen table, the backseat of the car, and hospital rooms turned classrooms. He took exams between seizures, with deadlines blurred by medication schedules and emergency admissions. He studied with ice packs on his head, read with one eye closed against blurred vision, and turned in assignments with trembling hands. To everyone's amazement, he was still earning straight A's.

And now—he was packing for another hospital, knowing full well he might take his next test hooked up to wires. He had every right to give up but didn't.

There was no room left in him for innocence: he looked like a teenager, but judging from the way he folded his clothes he could've been a soldier heading to the front lines.

I slipped in his favorite T-shirt with the faded graphic he wore on better days. My young Jedi.

We didn't know what would happen in South Florida.

We stepped forward with the diagnoses that finally named our battle, letting hope take the lead even when the way ahead remained uncertain.

Chapter 30

Jedi in a Hospital Gown

The world was panicking over a virus, but the battle I was fighting wasn't airborne. It had a name, a face, and a hold on my child so fierce it swallowed every other fear around it.

End of March, 2020. South Florida

Walking into the South Florida ER that night felt like stepping straight into a sci-fi thriller. The automatic doors hissed open and released a blast of sterile, icy air that hit my face like a warning—bleach, plastic, and something sharper that clung to the back of my throat. A security guard in a face shield blocked our way, no greeting, just:

"Do you have symptoms?"

I shook my head.

"We're here for our son, Michael Smith. His specialist preapproved and arranged appointments upstairs."

Behind us, someone coughed into their elbow while an alarm shrieked somewhere down the hall. Staff moved in a blur of gowns and fogged visors, their faces half-lost behind the layers, slipping through sealed doors with the quiet urgency of people fighting a war no one could see.

I wanted to be afraid of the virus everyone else feared, but fear already had its claws in me—and it wasn't named COVID.

I reached back and took Mikey's hand, feeling the faint tremor he tried to hide. We answered every question, held out the paperwork, and waited. The minutes dragged until a nurse from Neurology finally came down and confirmed what we had been trying to explain. Only then did the doors open.

Upstairs carried a different kind of fear. It didn't roar the way it did in the ER; it settled low, steady, almost disciplined, as if the whole floor understood the cost of panic. Warm light softened the corridor, and the pediatric room they brought us to felt unexpectedly human. Clouds brushed the ceiling in gentle strokes, blue walls eased the sharpness of everything we had been holding, and a small pull-out couch waited in the corner like a place where a parent could fall apart without judgment.

Only then did my lungs remember how to work.

And Mikey's did too.

From the first day, the staff felt like an answered prayer. They didn't skim his chart; they studied it, turning each page with the kind of care that tells a parent their child is not a task but a life. Their questions were precise, thoughtful, and rooted in a desire to understand rather than to hurry.

For the first time in a long while, Mikey felt heard.

They were there to help. Yet even inside that mercy, I caught the small truths that lingered at the edges: the way nurses changed their gloves with practiced urgency, the exhaustion etched into the doctors' faces, the quiet fatigue that no mask could hide. The room was gentler than the ER, but it was still a place shaped by suffering, built to hold bodies fighting battles they never asked for.

The infectious disease doctor looked as if rest had been optional for years, yet his presence steadied as he gave the diagnosis with quiet certainty:

"Bartonella." He said it like direction, not despair. "We'll start IV antibiotics right away."

Nurses moved with practiced ease as the line slid into Mikey's arm, and the atmosphere shifted just enough to breathe again.

We found small ways back to ourselves. A movie on the little TV. A joke whispered at the wrong hour. Laughter returning in thin threads but returning all the same.

When they began tapering one of the epilepsy medications, they did it with care, watching him closely, adjusting slowly. I noticed the IV line tremble when he rolled onto his side and thought how even hope comes anchored to something.

Quietly, in the space between his breaths and mine, the question rose:

Could this be it?

Could this *finally* be it?

Snolly Master

Mikey leaned over the Scrabble board, his grin pure mischief as he laid down his tiles.

Larry blinked. "Snolly? No way, Mikey! That's not a word."

Mikey didn't even look up. "It's short for snollygoster. Clever person. Triple word score."

Larry tilted his head. "That sounds like a cartoon character, not a word."

I laughed so hard my sides hurt. "Only you would pull that out, Mikey. Mr. CLEVER Pants."

For a few minutes, it didn't feel like a hospital room at all. It was just us, laughing until our cheeks hurt while Mikey demolished us with ten-dollar words and that smug little grin he saved for victory. He looked like himself again—eyes bright, wit sharp, shoulders loose—yet the pull of the IV each time he leaned forward reminded me how delicate the moment truly was.

We held on to it anyway, pretending laughter could hold the world together.

Later that night, while the monitors hummed and Mikey finally drifted to sleep, I glanced at the board still sitting on the tray table.

"Snolly," I whispered.

Just a word. But in that quiet, it felt like evidence that he was still in there. Proof.

The doctors kept pressing forward, each of them steady in a way that made it easier to breathe. The infectious disease specialist called with consistent updates, and Mikey's primary—our Iceland hero, icy on the map but all fire in spirit—sent every result the moment it was posted, chasing clarity with a focus that felt almost protective.

COVID pushed us out around day five, but this time, we left with a plan: antibiotics at home, a full schedule, coordinated follow-ups.

It felt less like a discharge and more like a handoff between people who actually *cared* what happened next.

When we stepped back into the Florida heat, the world outside still felt like it was burning—COVID raging, fear clinging to every surface. But inside our little bubble, we carried something different.

Hope roots deep in your bones.

I wanted to believe this was the moment we'd look back on and say, *That's when it started getting better.*

It almost was.

Chapter 31

The Gun That Didn't Go Off

W*here I come from, bravery often walks hand in hand with stupidity. That day, my father and I were both.*

Before the 1992 war came to our doorstep, my world was full of stories. I spent summers in the countryside, running barefoot through fields that held the bones of old battles. My cousins and I would gather around my grandfather—an old World War II survivor—with scraped knees and sunburned noses, sitting on wooden logs while he recited tales of Serbian heroes who had fought against the Ottoman Empire.

His voice would rise like a drumbeat, eyes twinkling as he embroidered facts with just enough fantasy to make us cheer.

We never knew which parts were real and which were invented, but we didn't care and we laughed anyway. He read to us, sent us on "missions," and taught us to cheer for the underdog. That was the beginning.

I loved books so much I'd get lost in them for hours, even if it meant chores went undone and spankings followed. The fairy tales promised happy endings, and I held on to them tightly.

At school, I was the girl who finished her homework early so I could help the ones who couldn't keep up. I remember one boy in particular—quiet, always tired, slumped in the back row with eyes too heavy for his age. No one paid him much attention. I did. Sometimes I'd slide into the seat beside him, whisper explanations, help him catch up. We became friends in secret. I never forgot the way his eyes would flicker with hope when he understood something.

Neither did he.

Unlike my mother—who was the smartest of five children but was forbidden to attend school because "girls cook, clean, and marry"—I went to college. I was the first girl in my entire family, on both sides, to do so. My mother was both proud and relentless and pushed me harder than anyone ever had. Even if it meant yelling.

"Don't you dare live a life like mine," she'd say.

Those words etched themselves into my heart, the way pain carves stone.

Keep Your Nose in the Books

I enrolled at the University in Sarajevo in 1989, bright-eyed with dreams bigger than the stigma that said school wasn't for girls. My neighbor-turned best friend-turned boyfriend dropped me off, reminding me (for the tenth time) to keep my nose in the books and not look at other guys.

"Study. Graduate early, so we can get married."

We didn't know it, but the war was already breathing down our necks. At first it was rumors and curfews, tension thickening the air.

Then came the Sarajevo wedding, March 1st, 1992. A newlywed couple walked out of a church, waving a Serbian flag. Gunfire broke the air. The groom's father was killed. Others were wounded. The city changed overnight. Lectures and books gave way to sirens and survival. Weapons began appearing in our dorms. One of my classmates pulled me aside."You need to leave while the roads are still open!"

The war was in full swing, cutting through lives like scythes through a field.

I was twenty-one, in my third year of college, when those blades cut through my own plans.

Car You Won't Need

After one of the bombings hit my hometown, the smoke was so thick you could taste it. Sirens blared, but the screams of the wounded were louder.

Bravery often walks hand in hand with stupidity, and that day, my father and I were both. We got in a car and started pulling bleeding bodies off the street. Some were barely breathing. Others begged us with their eyes, too far gone to speak. One by one, we loaded them into our tiny car—half-crushed, but it moved—and drove them to the ER praying we could get them there before breath slipped away.

The nurses knew our faces by then. They didn't speak—just nodded, eyes hollow, stepping forward to take the next body still clinging to life.

The hospital was overflowing: bodies on stretchers pressed shoulder to shoulder, the air sharp with iodine, sweat and fear. Cries rising above the beeping of failing machines became the last song of the souls breaking free from the body. Nurses shouted names no one answered to, and grief moved faster than medicine ever could.

We went back, knowing we might be trading places with the ones we were trying to save. The hospital disappeared in the rearview mirror.

Ahead—a checkpoint.

It hadn't been there ten minutes earlier.

We locked eyes. My father didn't speak; he didn't need to.

We both knew this might be the last time we saw each other.

"Step out of the car," one of the soldiers barked. "You won't be needing it anymore."

We stepped out slowly, calmly, because anything else might have been fatal. Then came the cold kiss of a gun against our foreheads.

This was it.

I've heard people say your life flashes before your eyes in moments like that…faces, laughter and scattered fragments of memory.

If that's true, it didn't happen to me.

I closed my eyes and braced myself for death, praying the sound I'd come to know too well wouldn't come from the one who raised me. I'd heard it so many times before—the body's cry when the soul abandons it—and it never got easier.

From dad, it would destroy me.

Years later, I heard that cry again. In a hospital that barely deserved the name. On another continent. From someone else I couldn't bear to lose.

And then—a voice.

"Put that gun down."

It cut through the tension like a blade.

"I know her. Let them go."

The soldier holding the weapon didn't move.

"I said LET THEM GO!"

Footsteps, authority in every step. Whoever it was, he wasn't just another uniform. He owned the space he walked in, like someone who'd seen enough horror to know when it had crossed a line.

"I know her," he said again, firm this time. "Put the gun down."

I opened my eyes, vision blurred with tears—and there he was: the tired-eyed boy from the back of the classroom only I ever seemed to notice.

He smiled, just enough for me to know he remembered. Our eyes exchanged the thank-yous our voices couldn't risk. The unlikely friendship between two kids divided by different religions met its most unexpected test in a war zone, with a checkpoint between us.

I didn't die that day, but I lost something: the illusion that safety is guaranteed, that the good guys always win, that justice always shows up in time.

That day, a bullet didn't kill me. But years later, in a fluorescent hospital hallway in Central Florida, another kind of weapon would.

And this time, the shot went straight through my heart.

Chapter 32

Between Miracles and Monsters

F*or the first time in 427 days, our son wasn't seizing. We should've been celebrating. Instead, we were walking into hell with lab results in hand.*

April—May, 2020.

Life after South Florida felt like the sun had cracked through endless clouds.

For the first time in over a year, life shimmered with hope. After endless seizures, frantic ER visits, nine failed medications, and neurologists who looked at our child like a riddle they couldn't—or wouldn't—solve, we finally had something real. No more guesswork and no more pills to quiet him. What we had now was hope, and this time it had numbers to prove it. Within two weeks of a simple dual-antibiotic treatment his seizures dropped by a staggering seventy percent.

Yes: s-e-v-e-n-t-y.

From dozens of episodes a week to barely one or two.

We felt alive again. We watched ridiculous spoof movies and laughed until our stomachs ached, tears running for reasons that, for once, weren't tied to fear. He requested meals and rated them like a food critic. Some days we managed genuine culinary wins; other days our humor was the main dish—and equally questionable.

Mikey:"Is this–bread?"

Me: "It's gluten and dairy-free... so, bread-*ish* enough."

Larry: "Close enough to fool a squirrel."

Mikey: "I'll allow it. But only if we never mention the zucchini pancakes again."

The house echoed with laughter again, and that was the only flavor on the menu that mattered.

He was still recovering, but we could *see* him now. He missed his friends, his chess matches, the driving lessons he had just started before the world collapsed beneath us, but he didn't dwell. He dreamed and started making lists instead.

"*When* I'm better, let's…" became his new mantra.

We were climbing out of the dark, one laugh, one meal, one ordinary day at a time. The pulse of the future was back in his veins—and ours. If anyone had asked us then, we would've said:

"This is the beginning of the end. We're finally out of the woods."

But hope, as we learned, can be a dangerous thing in the wrong system.

We didn't know we were walking into a trap.

By the third week of treatment, Mikey started acting…off. He'd get confused out of nowhere, look at things—at us—like they didn't quite add up. We figured it was the meds, or maybe his immune system kicking in. But the feeling in my gut—that one that never waits for proof—was already there.

We reached out to his primary.

"Check his ammonia levels," she said.

It sounded like something out of a biochem lecture, yet the labs confirmed what her instincts already knew: his ammonia levels were dangerously high. His confusion was a side effect of the antibiotics that were also saving his life. A cruel irony.

With COVID still strangling the health care system, our doctor couldn't admit him directly, so she sent us to Starlight Children's, the only place still taking patients. Like in South Florida, we had to go through the ER—not by ambulance this time, which we counted as a quiet win—but on foot, walking in with lab results in hand.

"We're here for elevated ammonia levels," Larry said, sliding the papers forward. "Per his physician's referral."

They admitted him to a general pediatric wing rather than ICU or neurology, and we clung to the idea that this meant it wasn't too serious.

We had *no* idea.

The walls were white, the air stale. A nurse smiled but didn't meet our eyes. A tech passed by holding a clipboard, glancing once, then quickly looking away. It should have felt like any other hospital room, but somehow, it didn't.

"Mom," Mikey said quietly. "I have a bad feeling about this."

I squeezed his hand. "It'll be okay," I said, trying to sound sure.

Somewhere deep inside, the same instinct that once told me to run during the war whispered again.

Something is wrong.

Chapter 33

Tall Cup of Suffering

7 *th hospital. 3rd floor, pediatric wing. Room 312. Day 4.*

May, 2020. Starlight Children's Hospital, Central Florida

A mother learns to hear danger in the tiniest things. A nurse avoiding eye contact. No doctors around—just too many residents. A question answered too quickly. That intangible static in the air.

"Mom..." He didn't even look at me, eyes on the ceiling. "I have a *really* bad feeling about this."

I didn't tell him I had it, too. What would've been the point?

My chest tightened with dread before the blow landed, knowing in my gut that betrayal isn't *if*—it's *when*.

"Tell me what feels wrong," I said, keeping my voice steady for his sake, not mine.

"They will hurt me here."

Mikey *knew*, with a certainty that broke me, that the harm would come from the very hands meant to mend.

I couldn't stop it either.
He lay there, awake, waiting for it.
"If it is possible, let this cup pass from me…"
It did not pass, and he drank it to the last drop.
All alone.

Chapter 34

Hush Little Baby, Hush

S*ometimes it isn't your own child's cry that tells you he's in danger—it's the sound of someone else's.*

May 20, 2020. Central Florida

There was a baby in the room next door who cried endlessly; not the restless whimper of a wet diaper, but something dark… like grief that didn't yet have words. The nurses said her parents rarely came. I never saw her face, but I longed to hold her, to press her against my chest, hum the lullabies I once hummed for Mikey. Tell her she was safe. Her sorrow seeped through drywall and doorframes, finding me in the silence where *my* screams should have been.

And then it struck me—I was the baby, too.

The IV pump clicked a steady metronome at Mikey's bedside. Plastic curtains breathed with the air-conditioning and the bed rail was cool under my forearms. He lay curled on his side, knees tucked, the sheet twisted around his shins. Hospital bracelets bit small grooves into his skin.

I slid the folder out from under my chair: our ledger, our

lifeline. I had printed spreadsheets at home—every seizure logged, every dose, every reaction. Arrows in the margins linked cause to effect the way detectives string thread between faces.

16 ER visits.

12 admissions.

1,421 seizures.

Numbers were the only way to keep the past from blurring.

A polite knock tapped on the door, and a resident stepped in with a smile that already knew the ending.

"Morning," he said. "How's our guy doing?"

He flipped through his chart—thin, safe, curated—and only then noticed the folder in my lap.

"What's that?"

"His records." I said. "It might help."

He took it by the corner, glanced, and offered it back as if it might stain his hands. "We don't really see Lyme down here," he said. "There's no Lyme in Florida."

The sentence buzzed through the room and landed where it pleased.

"There's also Bartonella diagnoses, confirmed by three different doctors," I said. "He got much better on antibiotics, seizures dropped by seventy percent. We are here for high ammonia levels from antibiotics."

"Bartonella isn't a real disease in humans," a second resident said from the doorway without looking up. "Cats get it."

Mikey stirred. "Mama?"

I leaned in. "I'm here."

"Water," he whispered.

I lifted the straw to his lips, and he took a sip like the cup weighed a hundred pounds. The male resident pulled the curtain back to look at Mikey again. "We'll have neurology swing by," he said. "In the meantime, we should consider discontinuing any meds that aren't… evidence-based."

"Evidence-based," I said, my voice a shade too bright. "Antibiotics reduced his seizures. Can you call the prescribing infectious disease doctor in South Florida, please?"

He smiled the way people smile at toddlers who say swear words. "We'll let *our* team decide."

When they left, their rubber soles said nothing.

The baby next door wound herself into another prophetic cry. I pressed my palm against my sternum and felt the old animal ache that had woken me in those first months of Mikey's life, before anything had a name.

He untucked his knees. "Mama… they will hurt me here," he whispered. "Please don't let them hurt me."

"They're here to help," I said, because that's what a good mother says, what a good mother believes. "I'm right here. I won't leave."

He nodded, eyes half-lidded, as if he had given me a job to do and was already forgiving me for failing it.

The door opened again. A new coat, a newer face, the badge turned backward. "We're reviewing his meds," she announced. "Given the lack of clear diagnostic support, we'll discontinue antibiotics for now."

My hands went cold. "The antibiotics are why he's getting better. The seizure drop—"

She held up a palm. "We're seeing no evidence for Lyme. And Bartonella—again, *not* a human pathology. Continuing is not medically indicated."

"The evidence," I said, and my voice went down a stairwell. "Is sitting in that folder and in his body."

Meanwhile, Mikey—my son, my miracle—was slipping again, but even then, his thoughts were never on himself. He worried about the crying baby, about me slumped in the chair, the nurses running thin, as if everyone else's burden mattered more than his own.

"Mama…" he whispered. "They will hurt me here."

"Can we get discharged, please?" I was trying to plead,

now *knowing* the storm was about to hit. "His ammonia levels are now in normal range, Covid is raging outside, and we would feel much safer at home."

"We don't think he's ready for the discharge, so, not at this time," she said.

Chapter 35

Discharge Denied

I *was ready to take my child home. They were preparing him for a coma.*

On day five, the actual neurologist walked in—our chronology in hand, pages worn, corners bent, streaked with highlighter. He settled into the chair with a gravity none of the others had shown. At last, someone listened without rushing, read without skimming, thought before speaking.

His verdict was blunt: Mikey was high-risk—dangerously high-risk—and we needed a home protocol for what to do if he stopped breathing.

"If he continues to seize… we may have to induce a coma."

Induce a *coma*? The words hollowed the air.

"Mama… I want to go home."

God, so did I. But when I asked about discharge *again*, they flat-out denied it.

Could they even do that?

I stepped into the hallway, pressed my hand to the cold tile, and slid to the floor. The ground opened beneath me.

This can't be happening. Not after South Florida. Not after the laughter, the food ratings, the hope.

Not after the staggering seventy percent drop.

From Bad to Worse

From there, it only grew worse. The antibiotics were stopped because they refused to believe the diagnosis. We were accused of "doctor shopping." The test results, the South Florida records—ignored. No consult was called.

No one cared.

And then, the blow that cut the deepest: They called Child Protective Services, insisting we were harming him with antibiotics because "there is no Lyme, no Bartonella." One phone call, and the stain followed us everywhere.

I was the enemy now, not the bacteria burning through his brain.

Not the arrogance leaving him worse with every hospital visit.

Somewhere down the hall, a cart squeaked. For a few breaths the baby next door suddenly got quiet. I leaned forward until my forehead touched the rail again. The metal was warm now.

Mikey's hand rose in the air, searching, and I met it with mine. He squeezed. I squeezed back.

Outside the door, voices moved around us, decisions braided and unbraided without us as well. Labels traveled faster than cures. Paper outpaced flesh. Somewhere a phone rang and was answered with a briskness that had nothing to do with care.

In the distance, the baby cried again.

Chapter 36

365 Days of May

I *'ve survived war. I've had a gun pressed against my forehead. But nothing—nothing—prepared me for what happened inside Starlight Children's Hospital in Central Florida.*

A place that should have brought healing, not horror, didn't just break protocol; it shattered his future, our trust, and the very idea that hospitals exist to heal.

It was early morning on Memorial Day Friday. No doctors in sight, only the uneasy silence that falls when those who should protect are absent. When the cat is away, the mice will play—and in this case, the residents took matters into their own hands.

The same one who doubted the Bartonella diagnosis stopped the antibiotics that were finally making a difference and pushed a high dose of a new epilepsy medication into his veins.

Immediately, seizures followed. I watched, powerless, as the medicine meant to heal only deepened his suffering.

His hands clung to my shirt, the only lifeline he had left. His wide, frightened eyes searched mine for the promise I couldn't keep.

Sleep-starved and aching, eyes raw from crying, every breath asked the same thing: Why won't they discharge us? The ammonia level is back in range.

So why the hell are we still here?

Chapter 37

Bruise That Never Went Away

H*is screams hit first. The fear came after. The bruise never left.*

May 22, 2020. 9:14 p.m. Starlight Hospital

Mikey was drifting off in my arms, when suddenly—without any warning—the door slammed open.

Four police officers rushed in like they were chasing criminals. Without a word of explanation, they began yanking me away from Mikey, ignoring his desperate screams—his terror—as if our bond, our pain, our love meant nothing.

All they said was, "You have to get out. Now!"

Larry and I stared at each other, waiting for the correction, the apology, the "wrong room." It didn't come. Only Mikey's bewildered screams piercing the silence:

"Mom, don't let them take you away! They'll hurt me!

"I knew something bad was going to happen! Don't leave! You promised. Mamaaaa!"

His voice cracked, raw with fear and desperation. I clung to him, my heart splitting in two. We held onto each other's hands like it was the last thing we'd ever do.

What if it was?

"Mama! This is what I was trying to tell you! Mama, please, come *back*!"

An officer finally forced me out of Mikey's arms. I kicked and screamed like a wounded animal, but his grip yanked me sideways and left a deep bruise on my right arm. It never faded. Never went away.

"Mikey! I called across the room. "This is just a misunderstanding! We'll be right back! Stay calm—be strong!"

One officer began shoving our things into a suitcase, another dragged me toward the door, and two held Larry back as if he were a threat.

"Officers, this is a mistake," Larry said, breath tight. "I demand to speak with someone in charge!"

Officer: "Sir, you need to leave. Now!"

"Mamaaaa!" Mikey cried.

"I'll be right back, Mikey!" I said. "I love you, baby! Please be brave!"

I kept crying out trembling promises that this was just a misunderstanding we could settle outside, and that I'd be back in no time.

But there was *no* time.

Whoever made that call—whatever soul they had—it was nowhere near that room.

Chapter 38

What About Mikey

W*hen they forced me out, I wasn't thinking about laws, or rights, or even myself. I was thinking one thing: What about Mikey?*

That forceful separation didn't just *feel* like destruction—it *was* destruction. Everything we were holding onto—our love, our faith, our sense of safety—shattered in one brutal, calculated motion.

They didn't just break our grip, they broke *us*.

The officers were spiteful for reasons we couldn't comprehend, but there was no time to process that now.

What about *Mikey*?

They dragged me out, one on each side, their expressions blank, their movements rigid. One yanked hard enough to twist my back, pain flaring through me as Mikey's screams grew louder behind me. A paper bracelet still clung to my wrist, proof we were once allowed inside.

I turned, desperate for one last glimpse, but all I could see was his hand reaching for mine, and I knew he hadn't let go. Not just yet.

The clock above the doorway kept ticking, loud and wrong, as though time refused to join the grief.

And then I heard it, his warrior cry.

A sound born in his soul, rotting in my bones. I've heard men scream in war, but this? This was worse.

Was it a seizure? Or did he just have a nervous breakdown?

Will I *ever* know?

One officer blinked, just once, as if remembering he had a mother. Then the mask slid back down and duty devoured decency again.

If Walls Had Ears

To this day, I still hear it, never knowing what caused it. Was it the high-dose medication the resident had given him earlier that made him worse? Or the trauma of witnessing a horror no child should ever see?

Or both?

All I know is that I didn't keep the promise I gave him, and he was all alone in that hospital, on that bed. Confused and terrified.

And what if that seizure—the one I wasn't there for—was *the* one they kept warning me about and I didn't even get to kiss him goodbye?

Never got to say I love you, just once more?

If I could've taken his place, I would've—a thousand times before morning.

And that, my friend, was just the beginning.

That cold gun from the war? In that moment, it finally went off.

Only this time, the bullet didn't aim for my head. It went straight through my heart.

Case Number, Not a Child

My heart didn't break; it was executed.

How many times, you ask? I don't know, I can't count that high.

They threw us out of the hospital room like trash and warned us:

"Do not come near the hospital."

I dropped on my knees, hands raised in helpless surrender, begging: "This is a mistake! *Please*, let us back in!"

But all I got was the cold smirk of a social worker who barked, "*I*'m in charge here."

Did I sign something wrong? Say something wrong? How fast can love turn into a threat?

She was still holding a clipboard. Someone always is.

Behind her, a janitor pushed a mop across the same floor where my son had just bled faith. The world kept cleaning itself while we shattered.

The verdict fell without a courtroom: "You are ordered to stay away from your son."

We were corralled like criminals, stripped of our dignity in the cold glare of indifferent eyes. Larry and I met in a gaze heavy with disbelief, words swallowed by the weight of what we'd just lost. Somewhere above the sirens, church bells rang the hour. I told myself maybe heaven was marking the moment, too.

I staggered backward, the roar of traffic rushing past like a storm, and only then did his voice break through the silence, fragile and raw: "I don't know what's happening."

Across the street, we stood—two parents exiled from their own child's bedside.

I straightened my spine. If they were watching, let them

see what faith looks like when it refuses to die standing on concrete.

If God truly counts every tear, I kept him busy that night.

The world kept moving, even when we couldn't. All that remained was the searing echo of his screams etched deep into our bones, and the blaring horn of a car narrowly missing the madwoman who stumbled into the chaos of the street.

That day, they didn't just turn my son into a number, a file, or one of hundreds of cases buried at the bottom of someone's inbox. They *stole* him from us, imprisoned him and branded all of us for life.

He was not just a case, a file or their number. He was—and forever will be—*my Miracle Child.*

You Can Check Out Any Time, But You Can Never Leave

We checked into the rundown hotel across from the hospital like ghosts haunting the scene of our own heartbreak. Mikey's desperate cries not to leave him kept echoing in my mind, sharp and relentless. On repeat.

That hotel became a last-ditch plea to stay close, to pull him back with nothing but proximity when presence was denied. To whisper without words: *We haven't gone far, baby. We're still here. Come back to us.*

Maybe—just maybe—someone would see reason and they'd let us back in. Maybe God would rewrite this cruel moment?

Larry was on the phone—who with, I can't say. Hospital? Lawyer? God? He wrestled with the impossible, his voice trembling, rising, falling, pacing the room just like his restless heart.

"Hey…do you know anyone who handles medical custody cases? Anything?"

A pause.

"No, this isn't about a bill. She's here. They threw us out. They wouldn't even tell us why."

He turned sharply, one hand in his hair, the other clutching the phone like it could hold us together. "I need someone who knows how to stop this. *Now.* Before they do something we can't undo."

I pressed my forehead against the cold glass of that sealed window, the invisible bars cutting through the air like a prison between us—trapping him inside, trapping me out. I clutched the empty space where Mikey's hand had been, refusing to release the memory of his touch.

What lesson could possibly live inside this kind of loss?

Down the hall, someone laughed, a sound too alive for a night like this.

Is he seeing the same sky out of his hospital room right now?

And then, like a thread pulled from a different war, a memory surfaced.

Chapter 39

The Prisoners of Hope

T*hree months before he disappeared behind hospital doors.*

February 6, 2020. St. Augustine

"Mom, tell me about the war you've been through!" Mikey's voice was full of innocent curiosity.

I looked at him, his eyes wide with wonder, as the wind danced softly through the trees.

"Some other time, my love," I replied gently. "The weather is so beautiful—let's just enjoy being outside. Let's enjoy the here and now. Look—let's watch the clouds."

He leaned back, eyes following a slow-moving puff across the sky.

"I wonder," he whispered. "What's the last thing someone loses?"

I paused. "Hope," I said. "Hope, my love."

Those who have ever been prisoners—of war, illness, fear, grief, or invisible battles—know it best: the thin flame you cup with both hands, afraid the wind will blow it out. And at the end of the day, isn't that what it truly is—the only light left to walk by, and the very thing the darkness keeps coming for?

~

And then—another memory broke through the madness, long before love—our fiercest weapon—was treated like a liability.

Mikey was only five, small enough to need help himself, yet already offering more than most grown people ever do. He carried light without knowing it, and love without trying to earn it. I didn't realize how much I would come to rely on both.

I'll never forget the store that day.

A small, elderly woman folded into a motorized scooter, moving slowly down the aisle. A can slipped from her basket and hit the floor, rolling just out of reach. She leaned over, stopped, tried again. Her hands shook and her fingers couldn't quite close around it.

I was a few steps away, still registering what happened, but Mikey was already there picking it up and placing it in her hands with a gentleness far beyond his years. He let his hands rest around hers, like he understood the moment needed more than a gesture.

She looked at him with a quiet kind of wonder, as if he had returned something far more important than what she dropped. A little hope, quietly stitched back together by the hands of a child who still believed kindness could fix what the world had broken.

He turned to me, glowing.

"Mom," he said. "I feel bubbles in my chest."

He didn't know how to name joy, so he gave it a name of his own.

~

Hope, Come Back

And that's who they took.

A boy who lived in light long before darkness ever claimed him. And still—they tried to cage what cannot be caged…

Mikey, in that very moment you taught me that even when the doors slam shut, hope bubbles up—quiet, relentless—a whispered promise that love is never truly lost.

I curled up on the floor beneath the sealed window, the invisible prison bars, across the street from the place holding my child hostage. The ache was unbearable. I couldn't see Mikey, but I prayed he could feel the fire of our undying love stretched across silence, across sorrow, across the street or any closed door.

Feel my hands still holding yours… and God's holding all three of us in the space where miracles still dare to breathe.

I wanted to grab the sky by the throat and scream him back into my arms.

Instead, I whispered to the silence:

"We are still here, Mikey. Across the street. Just a breath away. We haven't left you nor forsaken you. Not ever."

Hope… where are you?

Stay for the sake of the boy who still watches clouds and asks about war like it's something distant—not something he's living.

Chapter 40

Mama Bear Muzzled

They executed me without a crime. No coffin and no grave. Just a courtroom that pressed mute and called it procedure.

May 22, 2020.

I had promised Mikey—promised—that I would protect him, that they would have to go through me first.

But they didn't come through me.

They went around me, above me, behind my back… through the systems we once trusted, through loopholes no one warned us about… through secret meetings, signed forms, decisions made when we weren't even in the room. They ripped him away when he was finally starting to feel better, when we were just beginning to get a healthy version of my Miracle Child back.

They stole my son.

I stared at the hospital lights until they smeared, and my eyes felt like they were bleeding. I kept thinking if I looked hard enough, I could somehow get back to him.

The carpet felt like sand under my feet; I paced until the fibers wore thin.

They chose their moment with surgical cruelty—Friday night, Memorial Day weekend.

No one to answer to, no one to stop them.

Just silence. A mother's funeral without death.

And then it came: a phone call just before midnight.

Justice With Bad Wi-Fi

Emergency Shelter Hearing. 8:30 a.m. Central Florida.

May 23, 2020.

They called it a hearing, but no one wanted to hear us. No notice, no legal representation, no rights. Just a Zoom link.

The cursor blinked like a pulse I couldn't steady; boxes bloomed on the screen: titles, not faces. Justice, if you can call it that, arrived with bad Wi-Fi.

When I spoke, the sound died because someone, somewhere had clicked mute. A single button doing the work of a locked cell.

"Experts" who had never met my son, never read his chart, testified like prophets. Lies stacked on lies.

I kept raising my hand, but every system we're told to trust refused to hear me.

I stared at the screen, wondering if this was justice in America or the farce of a bad reality show.

The hearing kept moving, the way a river ignores a drowning. We were present, but our voices were not.

A kangaroo court in a browser.

Outside, morning kept happening.

Mikey's primary doctor, our Icy Fire, was in shock: "*How* could they do this?!" she asked, her voice shaking, as she pledged her support and offered everything that could help—records, witness. A kind word.

"They see what they want," she whispered. "Not what's real."

She knew what was happening wasn't just wrong: it was evil masquerading as protocol.

They used the word *shelter* as if tearing a sick child from a loving home were protection. They cast us as the danger. They mocked the antibiotics that had cut his seizures by seventy percent. They denied his diagnosis, calling it invention.

Then came the verdict they loved to hurl—Munchausen by proxy.

The judge blinked, just once, as if remembering he had a son. Then the screen froze, and the system swallowed mercy again. Justice was buffering.

They weaponized what I had learned for his sake, every scrap of research, every desperate attempt to understand, twisted into proof that I was harming him.

He *was* improving. I had watched him breathe like a child surfacing for air.

They forced him back under and called it justice.

All that was left was my own face staring back at the pixalated screen.

Chapter 41

Scriptures Under Covers

M*ikey became a prisoner of that hospital. Silenced by sedation. Everything that made him "Mikey"—his prayers, routines, his laughter, his courage, his voice—stripped away.*

May 23, 2020.

They wouldn't let him feel anything that reminded him he was still ours, so he learned to hide. He waited until they thought he was asleep, curled under hospital blankets, then texted us:

"I don't feel safe."

"Can you come now?"

"They said I'm not allowed to talk to you."

"Do we have time for at least *The Lord's Prayer*?"

That's how we communicated. That's how we prayed—over texts sent in fear, with trembling fingers and whispered scripture hidden under covers.

I didn't lose my faith that night, but we did have to hide it.

I never imagined we would have to smuggle prayer like contraband.

Not here.

Not in America.

Not in the Land of the Free.

Desperate Calls

May 22-May 26, 2020.

We called every day, sometimes three times, sometimes ten. Desperate parents begging to hear their son's voice, to hear how he's doing.

Sometimes they didn't answer at all. Sometimes they picked up just to hang up again, like Mikey was already gone and we were the last to find out.

"You're not allowed to call," they said, and hung up.

Our friend Jack found us a fierce, brilliant lawyer, ruthless in the way only a mother's desperation can inspire. It wasn't until Courtney stepped in that the line began to loosen. Even then, they gave only what they had to.

When we asked for updates, we were told someone would get back to us. No one did.

When we pressed for details, they said they didn't have them. The answers came only after the silence became a legal risk.

Courtney fought like hell.

She demanded supervised access. She dug her heels into the law and didn't even blink when the system tried to drown us in bureaucracy.

When doors closed, she found windows.

She even reached out to our priest's wife, Aleksandra, who submitted herself for a rushed background check so that someone we trusted could supervise our visits.

Then she showed me things they had written about me—hateful, twisted lies—so dark they rendered me unrecognizable, even to myself. Lies so vile that, if they had been true, *I* wouldn't have trusted me with my own son.

It wasn't a background check.

It was a character assassination.

Please Continue to Hold... Your Call Is Important to Us

We begged nurses for mercy, whispered voicemails through tears, left messages that sounded like 911 calls:

"Please check on our son, Mikey. 3rd floor, pediatric wing. Room 312."

"Please hold." Then the line went dead.

And then—somewhere in the middle of that chaos—a memory rose up and gutted me.

Only a few months before this relentless madness, Mikey had rehearsed with our choir, trying to muscle through the high notes without cracking. After the final *Amen* faded, someone tossed him a compliment—about his voice, his charm, or maybe just the fact he hadn't completely botched it. Without missing a beat, he smirked, straightened his collar, and said:

"Yeah, I know. I'm kind of a big deal."

Classic Mikey—equal parts cocky and hilarious, with just enough charm to get away with it. We all laughed, even the choir director, who shook his head and deadpanned:

"Don't let it go to your head, rock star."

That little moment—off-key singing, mischievous smiles, and laughter—was a bubble of joy I clung to like air in those fourteen days of hell.

And then, the bubble burst.

Chapter 42

Stolen Mid-Miracle

T*he worst part wasn't being told the rules. It was realizing they'd already been broken before we ever walked in.*

Once Courtney got on board, we were granted one hour a day with our son: sixty painfully short minutes. Supervised.

The social worker who met us in the hallway didn't introduce herself, no eye contact. She stood between us and the door like a checkpoint. Disapproval carved her face long before a single word was spoken.

"One hour," she said flatly. "Not a minute more."

Nothing could have prepared me for what was inside that room.

He was still in the same clothes we'd last seen him in, five days ago. Soaked in urine. The bed was soaked too. The room reeked of what appeared to be neglect.

He lay limp, skin the color of paper, IV lines snaking from his arm like questions no one would answer. The beeping was slow. Too steady. He was heavily sedated, like he'd already left the room.

I leaned over him, whispering, "Mikey… please… blink if you can hear me."

Without opening his eyes, he whispered back, "Mama… I *knew* you'd come."

And then, just like that, he slipped away again.

I sobbed quietly into his hand, hot tears falling between the IV lines and bruises on his arm. I kept whispering, "*I will bring you home.*"

The social worker never blinked. Her eyes were professionally blank, just like the report that followed: "Mother coaching him."

Can you even begin to imagine being accused of manipulation for comforting your child?

The one who whispered, *"Mama, please get me out of here."*

They confiscated his holy water and oil, and wouldn't let us pray with him at night.

We weren't allowed to call him.

Or hold his hand.

Or remind him that he wasn't alone.

They called it care.

The Hippocratic Oath

Adapted in modern language from the classical Hippocratic Oath (5th century BCE), traditionally attributed to Hippocrates.

I swear, by all that binds me to human dignity, to hold my craft as sacred and to serve life with integrity.

I will use my knowledge for the good of the afflicted, according to my skill and judgment, and I will do no harm.

I will not offer poison, nor counsel destruction. I will not raise my hand against the innocent, nor use my art to corrupt.

In every dwelling I enter, it shall be to heal, not to exploit.

I will speak no falsehood, share no secrets, and act not out of pride, but of duty.

May I live in honor, and may my hands bring no shame to the wisdom I have received.

But if I transgress and forswear myself, may the opposite befall me.

Somewhere along the way, they forgot the oath they took.

Chapter 43

We Forgot to Tell You

W*e showed up for a routine visit. Instead, we learned our son coded the night before—and no one thought to tell us.*

May 31, 2020.

I couldn't shake the feeling that something was wrong. Nothing specific had happened—that I knew of—but the anxiety kept escalating, refusing reassurance. I couldn't stay still. I kept getting up, pacing, sitting back down, every attempt at rest ending the same way. My mind kept jumping ahead to seeing Mikey again, louder and more insistent than usual, my body bracing for impact. At one point I found myself standing in the bathroom, hands on the sink, waiting for the feeling to pass. My instinct was making me nauseous. I puked.

Then came a call from Mikey.

He called us in secret, hiding under the blankets. I could hear the rustling. His voice was slurred and wet.

"Mama, the nurse took me for a walk… the floor was wet… I slipped…"

A pause. Then: "I hit the back of my head. Hard. There's blood… it's all down my face…"

"Can you see the blood?"

He was sobbing. I was screaming.

"I tried to call earlier, but they said no. No one helped me."

Then—footsteps. A muffled voice in the background.

"I have to go—"

Click.

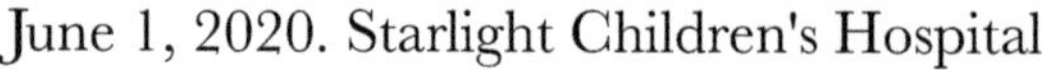

June 1, 2020. Starlight Children's Hospital

Nothing makes you feel powerless like the moment you realize the people holding your child also control the story of what happened to him. They decide *what* you're allowed to know, *when* you're allowed to know it, and whether you're allowed to matter. That morning, we walked into a hospital believing we were his parents. By lunchtime, we understood we were an inconvenience.When we arrived at his room the next morning, his bed was empty.

I collapsed and puked again.

"We've moved him to special care," they said, as if that explained everything. "You're not allowed in there."

The janitor stepped in to clean the floor. Her eyes found mine for a moment, carrying a quiet ache she hid the instant the nurse walked past.

We sat in our car outside the hospital for hours, waiting for someone to explain. *What unit was that?!*

Phones, once again, stayed silent. We were avoided like contagion, as if a mother's presence might infect the lies they were trying to preserve. It wasn't until we called our lawyer, crying and explaining they wouldn't let us see Mikey that they finally spoke… casually.

"Oh, yes… he had a little accident last night, hit his head… He coded, but he's stable now. He's in special care."

Wait—CODED?!

Special care?!!

As if they were updating us about a missed lunch tray. As if our son hadn't left this world for a few.

No explanation for why his parents weren't called when his heart had gone still. No apology, no urgency.

The truth?

Mikey's heart stopped the night before. In Central Florida.

After that phone call, mine *knew* something was wrong. From 103 miles away.

Can you imagine finding out—*after the fact*—that your son died and was brought back?

To realize you weren't important enough to be told?

To know that somewhere, under the blinding lights and among strangers, your child's spirit left his body—and you were not even allowed through the door?

Seventy times seven wasn't doing it.

I just couldn't find forgiveness for that.

The Camera They Wouldn't Show Us

We asked for the monitoring footage—the video of when Mikey fell or lay lifeless in the special-care unit.

They refused.

"Under review," they said.

"Being handled internally," they said.

They said everything except the truth.

Based on what Mikey told us, we came to believe a nurse had allowed a vulnerable, neurologically fragile minor to walk unaccompanied. And when he seized, he fell. Hard.

When his head struck the floor, when his brain misfired and his heart stopped—they failed to protect him.

And then they covered their tracks.

We will never know what really happened after Mikey was caught calling us and the line went dead.

I think about that moment more than I can admit. I imagine how the room must have changed the second they realized he had reached out, how their tone shifted, how the questions tightened. I come undone every time I imagine what those minutes felt like for *him* after he reached for us, scared and hurting and just trying to feel safe. Instead of comfort, he faced their anger for needing his parents. He faced it alone, blood on his face and fear in his chest, with no one who loved him allowed to stand beside him.

While in the special care unit, they put him on an IV medication already listed as an allergy.

They didn't call to ask if he had ever tolerated it, or if it had ever harmed him.

They just hung the bag and let a high dose run for too long.

The next PET scan showed spots on his brain he had *never* had before. We later learned those marks were from acute brain intoxication from *Dilantin* they kept giving him behind our backs. Our son has had seizures every day since.

Somewhere in that hospital, a camera recorded the truth.

We were never allowed to see it.

Another Letter to Mikey

Mikey —

I will not let this be the last thing you know. I will carry your laughter, the little jokes only we share, the way your hand fits in mine.

If the world forgets, I will not. I will write your name everywhere I can, whisper it when the nights are loud, and bring you home in every way I know how.

I write this for the day you ask—and for the day I can no longer keep silent.

To let you know who fought for you and how deeply, endlessly you are loved.

I do not know what you remember. I won't make you relive anything you cannot carry.

When the time is right, if you want to hear it, I will tell you the truth slowly, with room to stop. Until then: I keep your name a constant prayer on my lips. I pray for your healing.

And I promise: I will never stop fighting.

My love for you will endure this.

For you, for all of us.

Chapter 44

Mama, They Are Hurting Me

fter Mikey suffered a traumatic brain injury and coded on May 31, 2020, the hospital doors closed behind him.

We didn't see our son again until June 2.

He was *still* in the same clothes, the same smell clinging to him, the same unwashed sheets beneath him. Bruises covered his arms and legs. Even the bridge of his nose was swollen and darkening at the edges. His head was wrapped in tight gauze with fresh blood seeping through. His skin was ghost-pale, his body frail, his frame thinner than I had ever seen.

Larry quietly sat on the bed, reaching for Mikey's hand like letting go might shatter what little was left. Years of unshed tears broke the dam. The last time I saw my colonel cry like that was the day Mikey was born.

"I don't know how to protect you from something I can't punch," he whispered, his voice catching between anger and helpless heartbreak.

The rank, the distance, the hard edges he once wore like armor—gone. Only the father remained. The hands that once carried the weight of war now trembled for a boy he couldn't save.

I think Mikey heard him, and somehow—only God knows how—he smiled when his eyes recognized ours.

In that moment, his smile made the truth impossible to hide, the truth I had carried through every hour of those days while pretending I could survive it.

They had kept us from him.

And they had kept him from us.

But they couldn't break what held us together.

He reached for us with weak, trembling arms, and pulled us close. The boy who had coded just days earlier used what strength he had left to hug his parents like his life depended on it.

And it did.

"Mama," he said, "when can I come home?"

"Soon, my love," I told him, brushing the damp curls from his forehead. I said it like a promise, even though I wasn't sure I'd be able to keep it.

Then his voice sank, barely audible.

"Mama… they're hurting me. And there's this lady… she keeps coming, trying to get me to say you and dad are bad. She keeps asking me if you and dad hit me or yell at me. I told her she's wrong. I told her how amazing my parents are, but she gets upset when I say that."

They hurt my son in ways I can barely survive saying out loud, but the deepest wound they aimed for was the place inside him where we lived.

He protected that place with everything he had left.

Chapter 45

Slippery When Wet

E*ach day started with silence and ended with supervised permission to love my child.*

May 22—June 5, 2020. St. Augustine

No one warns you how loud silence howls when your child has been stolen from your home. It wasn't prison, but it felt like I was serving time just to hold my own child.

Days became a countdown. Every sunset carried the same ache, every sunrise brought us one step closer to the next time Sandra would pull into the driveway and take us to Mikey for another supervised visit. In the waiting—those cruel, hollow hours between visits—I prayed until prayer itself went numb.

One morning, she hesitated with the keys in her hand and whispered, "I don't know how you're standing on your feet."

I didn't know what to say to her… there just wasn't a word in the world for it.

But God.

I begged friends and family across the globe to join us in prayer for Mikey, and they did; at noon each day, voices of thousands rose like incense—different languages, different time zones, one desperate plea.

God's presence—undeniable.

Our prayers—unanswered.

Grandpa's Tears

My father stayed with us through that heartbreak, an old man raging against an unfamiliar war. He cursed American health care, spitting the words like venom.

"Heartless thieves," he said, his sharp Balkan accent cutting through the heavy air. He spoke the thoughts that stayed locked in my throat—not fit for a lady, and sure as hell not fit for the book.

My father didn't cry when he buried his father, nor when they lowered his brother into the ground, nor even in the frozen trenches where death breathed against his skin.

Now his tears carved deep lines into a face too weathered for this kind of softness. His hands trembled when he spoke Mikey's name—a broken whisper that seemed to shake the walls of the house.

Our tears made the floor slippery. Like mud.

My mind, traitor that it is, reached for Mikey's favorite kind—thick, sun-baked mud that squished between his fingers like joy refusing to die.

Mud and Mischief Memory

Eight-year-old Mikey, St. Augustine

Some kids build castles out of sand.

Mikey built kingdoms out of mud.

Mikey and Brooke—his wild-hearted, mud-and-lizard-loving partner-in-crime—seemed to carry trouble in their back pockets. On hot afternoons, they'd come inside caked head to toe in mud, grinning like swamp creatures on their lunch break—Brooke with a lizard on her shoulder, Mikey with a frog held like he was some uncrowned prince. I nearly passed out when I noticed a worm curled between his toes.

I stared at them. "Should I even ask?"

Brooke sighed. "We slipped."

"Correction," Mikey jumped in. "*She* slipped. I was collateral damage."

I raised an eyebrow at the frog. "And this one?"

Mikey lifted it like proof. "He's fine."

"You're both banned from indoors until college."

Out came the garden hose—again.

For one flicker of time, I let the memory stay: Mikey chasing Brooke with a handful of worms. Brooke spraying him with the hose in retaliation. Mud flying, frogs cheering them on in spirit. Sunlight hitting their faces like the universe gave them a standing ovation.

Like the world had forgotten how to be cruel.

And then it was gone, leaving me wandering through rooms that still remembered Mikey, my eyes landing on the empty couch where his presence should have been.

The house held him everywhere except where I needed him most.

I lit a candle and dropped to my knees before the icons, my forehead pressed to the same wooden floor that once held his feet when we stood there together, our voices braided in evening prayer.

And there, on my knees, I felt him close enough to steady me for what was coming next.

Chapter 46

14 Days of Hell

I *kept waiting for a miracle. What came instead were fourteen days of silence so thick I forgot what mercy sounded like.*

Seconds scraped like glass under my skin; there was no morning, no night anymore. Time lost its rhythm. Clocks ticked out of step with reality as sunrise and sunset collapsed into one endless gray. We were trapped in our own home—without him.

My body didn't know where to store the pain, so it broke out in sobs, screams, and long, frozen stillness—on the kitchen floor, in the hallway, against the refrigerator, on the cold bathroom tile. Even the hum of the refrigerator sounded like grief.

I dry-heaved.

I tore through drawers like a madwoman, searching for something that still smelled like him. I buried my face in his shirt until it was soaked through with tears.

"God, *please*. Let me hold him. Let him live. Take *me* instead."

We kept setting his place at the table and making his bed

as if at any moment he might walk through the door. As if pretending hard enough could force the nightmare to break.

But it didn't. It stretched on. Every time the phone rang, my chest caved in with panic.

Was *this* the call?

I would have burned the whole world down for five more minutes with him. Grief and terror lived in every corner of the house, in the paint on the walls, the air, under the skin I wore.

I pray you never bear the memory of a child dying alone because the law kept your hands tied.

To be told you have no right to ask if he is still breathing.

Silence became our constant companion.

Even love couldn't find its way through it.

I regretted marrying Larry too many times to count. Pain always looks for somewhere to land, and the closest heart is often the one it wounds first. While we were separated from Mikey, I couldn't stand the sight of Larry.

The weight of everything we were carrying pressed down so hard that love no longer felt like love. It felt like a mistake I couldn't undo.

I remember staring at him through tears that burned more than they fell, thinking, *If I hadn't married you, maybe I wouldn't be standing here in this heartbreak. Maybe I wouldn't know this kind of pain.*

Grief is cruel that way. It doesn't care who it cuts, only that it finds a place to bleed. And in those hollow, unbearable moments, the man who once felt like my safe place became the mirror reflecting everything I had lost.

We were alive, but we weren't living.

Chapter 47

Chorus of Witness

T*hey took him without proof. We took him back with facts.*

June 5, 2020. The Day the Silence Broke

We got him back on June 5. Fourteen days of unimaginable terror, of waiting, of praying with fists clenched and phones unanswered, locked outside the system's doors with nothing but despair.

Three hundred twenty-seven hours of hell.

It was the same court, still boxed inside that cold Zoom window. The same judge, unmoved then, unmoved now. We sat a hundred miles away, still nowhere near Mikey's bruised, drugged body fighting for life.

Two weeks ago, they called an emergency shelter hearing against us.

This time around, the emergency hearing was ours.

Our lawyer demanded it, fought for it, and after two relentless weeks it was granted. She stacked the record with dates, meds, scans, and contradictions so stark they forced the court to face what it had tried to ignore.

The "experts" who'd never met our son were forced on the record, to speak in specifics.

Silence wasn't a weapon that day; it was the room holding its breath while the truth was read aloud.

Our lawyer laid out the violations one by one: protocols ignored, laws broken, permanent physical and emotional damage inflicted on a boy who should have been safe. She obliterated the state's case.

Courtney: "Doctor, can seizures be caused by Lyme disease?"

Expert: (hesitates) "Well, typically—"

Courtney: "Yes or no, Doctor?"

Judge: (stern) "Answer the question."

Expert: (quiet) "Yes."

Courtney: "Can an EEG pattern that looks like epilepsy be caused by an infectious or inflammatory process?"

Expert: (shifts) "In some cases—"

Courtney: "Judge, may we have a clear answer?"

Judge: "Answer."

Expert: "Yes."

Courtney: "So it is possible the abnormalities we see are not classic epilepsy but a secondary effect of infection?"

Expert: "Yes."

(beat—the Zoom courtroom exhales)

Clerk: "Call the next witness."

Dr. Taryn: "I have treated Mikey. I've seen his response to antibiotics. I have watched seizures decrease. I stand by my chart."

Mikey's therapist: "Their claim that the home was harmful is untrue. I assessed the family dynamics and found care, not neglect."

Courtney: (holds up a letter) "And though our Lyme specialist could not be present, his letter is in the record."

Clerk: (reads) "Dr. Steinberg—clinical opinion: infectious etiology likely; treatment response consistent with infection-mediated neurologic dysfunction."

Courtney: “Undeniable.”

Outside, prayers rose from Florida to Europe: church groups, Bible-study sisters, my lawyer’s quiet prayer before we started. Every text, every candle, every whispered psalm, a rope pulling us through. In that chorus of witness and prayer, the judge ruled…

“Return custody to the parents. Effective immediately.”

Chapter 48

But My God Did

W*hen the order came, it was the correction. The same system that silenced us now had to speak.*

June 5, 2020.

"Start driving," our lawyer said. "I'll have everything ready by the time you get to Starlight Hospital."

We grabbed the keys and walked out fast, as if the house itself pushed us forward. Reaching him was the only direction left.

The traffic, the horns, my breath—everything disappeared beneath one name pounding through my chest like a war drum:

Mikey. Mikey. Mikey.

When we finally reached the hospital, morning waited for us with a sky too bright for what we were walking into. The parking lot stretched wide and empty, but none of it registered. I couldn't feel the sun, only the distance between the car and the boy I had fought so hard to keep safe. Each step toward that building felt heavier than the one before it. My legs moved, but it was the memory of him that carried me forward.

Ghost Town

Once in that hospital, we burst through the doors that—this time—offered no resistance. The hallways were hollow, the nurses' desks abandoned. Faces ducked behind partitions and doors clicked shut, as if we were ghosts returned to haunt them.

I didn't care.

Their greetings meant nothing, their absence even less.

The path to him was already carved into my bones. And when I reached his door, there was no knocking, no pause—only a mother crossing the threshold from which she never should have been barred.

There he was, tangled in blankets that offered no warmth, a shadow of the boy he'd been only weeks before. Curls stripped of their attitude, limbs slack, a face carrying years he hadn't lived.

Seeing him like that cracked through every defense I had left. Even in that state, a part of me rose like the first time I held him, certain he was still here and still mine.

He was ours again.

"Mama?"

I dropped to my knees beside him and laid my hand against his cheek, brushing back the hair that hadn't been cleaned. I spoke softly, not wanting the moment to be louder than it had to be. I held his hand like I was afraid it might disappear:

"We're here, baby," I whispered through tears. "We are busting you out."

His eyelids fluttered, then slowly opened. His gaze met mine through the sedation, and even in the haze I saw the boy I raised, carrying more knowing than his years should have held.

"Mama… I prayed the whole time," he whispered.

Tears spilled before I could stop them.

"I was on my knees for hours during the hearing, whispering *I can do all things through Christ who strengthens me.*"

I leaned in, forehead to forehead, holding his hand, not wanting to let go. Not now. Not ever.

He blinked slowly, and then said the words I will never forget:

"I couldn't… *But my God did.*"

That's when I exhaled.

This was him—his voice, his eyes, the strength still alive beneath everything they'd tried to strip away.

They thought they were right when they took him, but he was never theirs to hold.

What they underestimated was our God.

Chapter 49

What the Hospital Sent Home

W*e thought the worst was over the moment we carried Mikey out of that hospital, not realizing we were walking straight into another war.*

Life After June 5, 2020.

Mikey's trauma stamped deep. He was paying the price for battles he never chose.

Larry retreated into himself, burying fear in endless work—and in the whiskey bottle that lived on the counter, emptier each morning than the night before. Sometimes I'd hear the soft clink of glass in the kitchen after midnight, a sound that told me his fear was no quieter than mine.

And me? It felt like something inside me had died, but I couldn't tell anyone. I was painfully aware of my helplessness. I still had to work, because the "love letters" from hospital billing departments never stopped coming. The stack of unopened envelopes on the counter stared back like accusations, each one a reminder that life marches on, indifferent to our pain.

Lying awake, staring at the ceiling, my mind screamed:

How do you pick up pieces of what once was and pretend it didn't happen?

Chapter 50

James Bonding

P*eople say adrenaline lets you lift a car. But no one tells you that, when it's gone, you can't even lift yourself. Sometimes the heaviest weight is your own heart.*

June, 2020. St. Augustine

The medications stole his spark. Words came slow and heavy, like they were wading through syrup. Larry and I slept on the floor beside his bed, a canyon of exhaustion between us, both waking at every change in his breathing.

Once home, we tried to be more upbeat and fill the hours with something that didn't hurt. Our laughter was the only thing their pills couldn't quiet.

"Let's binge all the James Bond films," I said one night. "We'll call it… BONDING. James Bonding."

He gave me the classic teenage eye roll that used to mean we were going to be okay.

"Why does he always say his name twice?" he asked with effort. "We get it, bro. You're Bond. No one else is applying for the job."

"Maybe it's his pickup line," I said.

He threw a handful of popcorn into his mouth. "Imagine

him at the grocery store—'Name on the loyalty card?' 'Bond. James Bond.'"

We laughed until we wheezed.

For a few minutes it felt almost normal—our laughter bouncing off the walls, the smell of popcorn hanging in the air, Oreo's tail thumping against the floorboards.

Then the scene changed.

Bond was trapped behind bars, stripped of his weapons, villains taking turns interrogating him—pressing, twisting, demanding answers. The room around us fell quiet. Mikey's grin faded. His voice came soft, almost flat.

"Mama… this is how I felt. It was a prison. I didn't get to say or do anything. They kept coming, trying to get me to say things that weren't true."

The popcorn bowl slipped from my lap, kernels scattering like tiny explosions across the floor. Larry froze, eyes fixed on the screen. I wanted to reach for Mikey, but something in his stare told me not to interrupt.

The television light flickered across his face, and I realized the movie wasn't entertainment anymore. It was memory.

He blinked once. Twice. Then looked away to hide tears.

I swallowed hard. "Oh, the sting," I whispered—but it wasn't about the movie anymore.

That night I understood what no diagnosis or court document ever captured: The real interrogation never ended. It just changed rooms.

The credits rolled, but the light stayed on.

Chapter 51

We Still Count the Tears

Some wounds never make it into the medical record. Some verdicts never reach a courtroom. But they sentence you just the same—and you still serve the time.

I once believed the worst was behind me. That the sound of sirens and shellfire belonged to another lifetime, another world. That the war that tore through my country had finally spent its fury.

I was wrong.

This war didn't come with bombs; it arrived in pressed scrubs, polite smiles and paperwork. When it cut, it left no visible wound. When we bled, they blamed us for bleeding. Then asked for our insurance.

I held Mikey and wept—not just for what we endured, but for the slow, sickening realization that this wasn't an innocent mistake. It was a system working exactly as designed. Built to break people without leaving fingerprints.

How many others, I wondered, were quietly broken—wreckage hidden behind locked doors?

I used to believe the system—however flawed—was at

least trying. That somewhere behind the forms and signatures there were people who cared. But that belief died quietly.

In Yugoslavia, it was neighbors turning away. Here, it was institutions doing the same. Different uniforms, same blindness.

Behind the curtains, medical students made irreversible decisions without oversight; behind courtroom doors, judges silenced evidence that didn't fit the narrative; behind logos and polite words, caseworkers stopped seeing our son and only saw a file.

We weren't punished for harming our child. We were punished for loving him.

For all the families erased, mine became the example.

I will never forget the physician from NE Florida. His face is gone from memory, but that pinky nail remains—long, polished, sharpened for show. It told me everything he never had the courage to say out loud. He wasn't here to help.

When Starlight kept blocking every attempt to discharge Mikey, we turned to him, pleading for a transfer into his care. The moment he heard Child Protective Service got involved, he denied the transfer.

Then came his letter:

"You are no longer under my care."

Then came the silence.

It's strange how quickly a life can be reduced to paperwork and how fast compassion turns procedural.

Friends stopped calling. Some of the patients at my practice never came back. Colleagues avoided my eyes. Even people we had asked to supervise visits with Mikey suddenly pulled back, without a word.

Once I had been a physician. A mother. A friend.

Now, I was a headline no one wanted to read past.

DCF doesn't apologize. CPS doesn't retract. Once they mark you, they walk away, leaving a family to choke on ashes.

My tears fell in places no one thought to look: in the dark corners of parking garages, behind the linen closet door, into the folds of my hands when the world wasn't watching. Some prayers never made it past the steering wheel; the car became my confessional, the only place I could fall apart without consequence. I have groaned louder than language.

I have held my son while crying, and I have cried while being kept from him.

Grief has no bottom. And trauma doesn't end just because the paperwork does.

In spite of it all, we survived. Not because justice woke up or the system corrected itself. We survived because even on the days when hope limped and faith trembled, love held the line.

It endured. It always does. Even when everything else fell apart.

And if these pages found you—if any part of this story settled into the places you don't show the world—then you already know this much is true:

Love endures in you, too.

Chapter 52

He Walked Anyway

A *fter years of fighting for his life in places meant to save it, the day we once believed was impossible finally arrived: High School Graduation.*

May 26, 2022. St. Augustine

No extended family flew in, but the ones who had chosen to be family all along came to lunch with us. We went to the same restaurant where half the city had shown up for his Sweet Sixteen—only this time, he didn't remember *any* of it. That memory lived in us now.

Two celebrations, layered over each other like an old photo pressed into a new frame. One remembered. One lost. Both soaked in love.

Then it was time.

The amphitheater buzzed, every seat humming with anticipation. One student after another made their way across the stage, applause rising and falling. When they called Mikey's name, the whole place erupted, cheering him forward as if his journey had lived in them, too.

And there he was.

Tassel swinging, chin lifted, face steady.

Standing tall and stepping forward as if the stage—and this moment—had always belonged to him, no matter how many times the world insisted it didn't.

Shoulder to elbow, Ms. Eloise walked beside him. She had been his gifted teacher since elementary school and when Mikey was placed in the hospital homebound program, she immediately volunteered to be the liaison teacher between school and home. And now she walked with him at graduation, her very presence saying, *"Try him, and you'll answer to me."* She marched stride for stride, like she'd been fighting for this day, too.

Phones flashed. The wind lifted his tassel. I don't remember other faces.

Only Mikey's.

When the principal placed the diploma in his hands, he announced, "With honors," as if naming every mountain Mikey had climbed to reach that moment.

And Mikey, steady as ever, gave a half-smirk and said:

"Don't tell my neurologist. He still thinks I can't read."

He gave that signature shoulder roll, the one that always said, *I've got this.*

And then the cheers—loud, wild, earned. The moment was big, but he was bigger.

Larry and I both cried the fast, ugly and joyful tears that tasted like grief and glory at the same time. We weren't just crying for the moment but for all of it—the seizures, the hospital nights, the moldy walls, the meds, the system, the fear, the ache. Every weight collapsed into that roar of applause.

The noise faded, but the moment never did.

I watched the friends who had carried hope beside him all these years sweep in around him.

Lila hugged him so hard his cap fell off.

"You did it," she whispered, half-laughing, half-crying.

Nearby, his friend John stood, shaking his head like he couldn't believe what he was seeing.

And me?

I sat in the crowd, hand over my mouth, tears streaming, staring at the boy who refused to be erased. My son—who danced through trauma, diagnosis, red tape, and near-ruin—walked across that stage.

What he really walked through was hell.

And he walked anyway.

Part IV: Shattered Hallelujahs

Chapter 53

The Crash That Broke Everything

F*our hundred ninety-two days after they tore us apart, the world crashed again.*

September 27, 2021.

The light turned red, two minutes from the church parking lot. Mikey in the passenger seat, curls against the glass. Larry in the back, steady hands ready if the moment called for it. For a heartbeat, everything was ordinary. Then—

BOOM!

A sound that split the world open. Metal screamed. Glass exploded. We were thrown forward, then sideways, then back again—caught in slow motion, slow enough to wonder if time is mercy or mockery.

When the noise stopped, silence roared louder.

We looked at one another—hands, faces, pulse checks of disbelief.

"Are you okay?"

"Are *you* okay?"

"What just happened?"

Larry bolted from the car. No one behind us. The traffic

kept moving, drivers craning necks, irritated that our wreck was in their way.

I couldn't feel my body. Mikey was too quiet. Larry, wired with adrenaline, shouted, "We got hit! Hit-and-run!" as he dialed 911.

Seconds folded into minutes, minutes into silence. I remembered how quickly they'd arrived the night they tore our family apart at Starlight Children's Hospital. That memory pulled me under, back into what never truly ended. But now? When we needed them? Nothing.

When the officer finally arrived, he barely looked up from his clipboard.

There's always a clipboard.

"Yeah, hit and run. Here's your report, call your insurance."

No witnesses. No help. No humanity.

Pieces of the car scattered like breadcrumbs on the asphalt. Somehow, numb and foggy, I drove us home.

Aftermath

The next morning, we sat in the quiet room of our doctor's office. Three concussions—one for each of us. Several broken bones as confirmation of what I already knew: *we were already broken.*

A few days later, Mikey was airlifted to the same children's hospital that had pushed the first medication that made everything worse.

When they finally ran the test I begged for, it confirmed what no one wanted to admit: Depakote *was* triggering more seizures, and he couldn't metabolize it at all. The whole "It's the natural progression of epilepsy" and "You're obstructing medical treatment, ma'am" fell apart under the weight of one set of results.

Turns out, I wasn't obstructing treatment. I was a mother who knew her child.

I knew.

And now we were back, surrounded by faces we had learned to fear.

I hated them.

~

Larry drank to keep the world quiet. Every night the bottle did the talking he wouldn't. When grief hit, the drinking got worse, and so did our fights. I held our life together with whatever strength I had left.

The visible wounds were bad enough; the invisible ones ran deeper.

Headaches cracked through my skull like lightning. Tears came without reason, rage right behind them—I was a live wire with no insulation left. I fell constantly, whether from the concussion or trying to break Mikey's fall during a seizure, new breaks stacking over healed ones. The pain was its own kind of punishment.

I couldn't stand God. But I missed Him, too.

I stopped going to church. Even the priest—kind, patient—grated on my last nerve.

He'd say, "Bear your cross with dignity. Rejoice in your suffering...."

What did *he* know?

What did *any* of them know?

Mosquito in the Dark Room

I called the sheriff's office every single day, begging them to check the traffic cameras. That intersection was covered from every angle. Someone had to find the driver who nearly killed my entire family—the man who knew what he'd done but chose to flee.

"We're busy," they said.

Why wouldn't they just look?

I was a mosquito in a dark room that no one could swat until, finally, the officer was told to pull the traffic footage.

And there it was: a car flying over sixty miles per hour, didn't even tap the brakes, slammed into us, and just kept going.

An arrest warrant. Finally.

But too late. My family was already falling apart.

Chapter 54

No Justice. Again.

The police told us they wouldn't pursue charges. With public pressure around race and law enforcement, they didn't want the optics of an arrest.

"It's complicated," one officer said.

I understood the climate, but to us, it wasn't complicated at all—he hit our car, fled the scene after he nearly wiped out the entire family, then got away without a single consequence.

The system that should have protected us chose to protect itself. Again.

Sound familiar?

The first breaking happened at Starlight Children's, the night they pulled Mikey from my arms and silenced my voice. That night I learned that love wasn't enough to protect my son in a system that refused to see the truth.

The second breaking came slower.

My body rejected every prescription they tried, so I chose pain over haze. Sleep disappeared, and all the pain stayed.

I carried it like armor. It was the only way I could keep carrying Mikey.

Chapter 55

Same Weapon. New Body.

M*y parents came to help with Mikey. They ended up saving me.*

December 16, 2021. St. Augustine

When they flew in from Bosnia that winter, they walked into a home held together by a daughter who could barely stand. I was sleep-starved, limping through the days, eyes hollow from pain and nights without rest, but still upright, still pretending I could carry the weight that had already broken me twice. I kept telling myself I could endure it.

Until I couldn't.

Another seizure tore through Mikey in the night, and when it finally released its grip on him—on us—I staggered into the next room and collapsed onto the floor. Larry stayed beside Mikey, watching for the next wave. At that point, we never knew if it meant one seizure or another 911 call. That was our reality.

My sobs started silently, then broke open, violent enough to twist my stomach and split my skull with pressure.

This was the night my strength reached its limit.

By five a.m., I was shaking, dragging myself from the floor to the bed. I texted Larry, still guarding Mikey:

"Taking Tramadol for pain. The pain has become unbearable."

One small, round attempt at relief. And a brutal way to learn I was allergic to the medicine meant to help me.

By dawn, I was "locked in." I could hear everything but move nothing. Larry thought I was finally resting, but my father knew better. He barged in and shook my motionless body, shouting for Larry. My mother cradled my head, whispering in broken Serbian:

"Wherever you are...please come back. Don't you dare leave us."

The ambulance came—this time for me.

They saw what they wanted to see: pill bottles, labels, a story they filled in before speaking to either of us. They lifted my prescriptions like trophies, like evidence of a crime.

The paramedics ignored Larry's frantic explanations and the text still open on his phone.

He fought for me.

"She doesn't take them. She can't handle medication. She would never overdose."

They didn't hear him.

They didn't care.

Mistaken Addict

At the ER, the cruelty deepened. Nurses got irritated by my mother's broken English, sneering at her tears. A doctor shoved a tongue depressor into my mouth, muttering–in his own, strong accent–"Strange..."

I wanted to scream, "I'm alive. Please stop." I was trapped, a prisoner in my own skin.

One of the nurses insisted she'd seen me before—a drug addict who had overdosed again. I heard every word but couldn't move, couldn't scream that she'd mistaken me for someone else.

Larry's voice cracked. "She can hear you. Look at her tears!"

The nurse didn't even glance at my face. "She overdosed."

Larry stepped closer, desperate. "You don't know her. She wouldn't take medication—she can't. Please, listen—"

"Sir, step back," the nurse snapped. "Leave now or we'll call security."

They forced Larry out.

The room held its breath.

Then—Narcan, meant to save overdose victims—an overdose I didn't have—ripped through me like fire, searing my chest, scarring my heart. My organs began shutting down, one by one.

Someone shouted, "She's seizing!"

I wasn't seizing.

I was dying.

One by one, the lights inside my body flicked out. Their ignorance was killing me, too.

Same weapon. Different body.

This time, mine.

Chapter 56

Cheesy Love

M*y body started to drift; I couldn't tell what was real anymore.*

I thought I heard my mom cry outside the door, calling my name. My sweet mom. Such a rough life, but such fierce love.

And humor.

The kitchen always came alive around her. Food was her love language, and we always left her visits feeling five to ten pounds more loved. She made *burek* the way she always had—by feel, not recipe—folding dough with her fingers, brushing oil like it meant something. The smell alone brought tears I couldn't explain.

Mikey wandered in mid-morning, sniffed the air, and blinked like someone's grandma just slapped his soul with a wooden spoon.

"Is that cheese?"

"It's burek," I said. "Your grandmother's recipe."

"AND cheese?" he repeated.

I nodded.

He grabbed a slice and ate standing up. Then another. Then two more. He didn't stop until he was leaning against the fridge like it might hold him upright.

He closed his eyes and whispered, full of drama: "If I don't make it… tell Nadia I loved her."

My mom muttered something in Serbian without turning around.

Mikey clutched his stomach. "Also tell my stomach it brought this on itself."

I passed him a napkin. "It was the cheese."

He nodded. "It was worth it!"

Laughter.

And then — nothingness.

Owner of a Broken Heart

For three days, I lay intubated. Machines breathed for me, tubes kept me alive. My body—broken, unresponsive—was carried on the prayers of others.

When I finally opened my eyes, it was nothing short of a miracle.

But nothing was the same.

My heart bore new scars. (*I learned that "Broken Heart Syndrome" was a real thing.*) My spirit bore new cracks. So did my faith.

A system sworn to heal had nearly buried me, too.

For a moment, the dove appeared—hope, faint but real.

And then the devil followed.

Chapter 57

After the Dove Came the Devil

"B*ut wait, there's more!"*

Summer 2022. St. Augustine

That same accident had left Mikey weaker too. Seizures kept coming—harder, faster. God remained silent, and that made me feel so completely, unbearably alone.

We found a doctor in south Florida offering IV therapy that *might* help Mikey. That meant packing bags, planning every detail so Mikey could tolerate the trip. Hotels. Days of therapy. The long drive home. By then, my parents had flown back to Bosnia, and we were on our own again.

While we were gone, the water heater burst, flooding our house—five days straight.

How much longer, God? *Seriously!*

Insurance shuffled us into a hotel for months. Contractors didn't show. Stress stacked higher and higher until it pressed against my chest like a weight I couldn't lift. Mikey's fragile routine collapsed—no clean kitchen, no ability to stick with routine and his dietary restrictions.

Three months later, stepping back into our house felt like relief. Like maybe, just *maybe*, we could exhale.

Then hurricane season hit. And, of course—we lost the roof.

Workers promised help, took our money, then vanished. Stress layered on stress until every day was another stone crushing me. Hotels were full. Nowhere to go. Nowhere to hide. *Maybe I should've pitched a tent on the courthouse lawn and called it poetic justice.*

I had nothing left to give, but life kept demanding more.

And that finally broke me.

Pain ruled my body. Fear ruled my nights.

One hospital after another. One talk of divorce after another.

I lived in agony. Physical pain. Trauma. I was barely able to work, only to come home to a drunk husband every night. I was trapped in a body that didn't feel like mine, in a life that no longer belonged to me. I stopped praying altogether and started spitting snakes at God with blazing, consuming anger.

I was sick and tired of seizures. Of endless suffering. Of a marriage breaking apart one silent night at a time.

And of God who went out for cigarettes and never came back.

Gone.

Chapter 58

Major Fall and a Minor Lift

T*hey say every Hallelujah has a minor fall and a major lift. Mine began with four words I never thought I'd say: I didn't care anymore.*

If hell had doors, I was already through them. Death didn't frighten me; it started to sound merciful. *What kind of Father lets children burn while mothers kneel?* I wanted to believe.

I just didn't know how.

The verse *"The fool says in his heart, 'There is no God'"* came back to me like a mirror that night. Not because I believed it, but because I was standing one breath away from becoming it.

Faith had become a foreign language I couldn't speak anymore. My prayers went unanswered. If heaven had a dial tone, mine had long gone dead.

And when God goes quiet long enough, you start listening to other voices.

I Turned to Fortune Tellers Instead of Prayer

My Shepherd was nowhere to be found, and this strayed sheep finally got devoured.

I turned to fortune tellers and their cookies. Deep down I knew it was wrong, but anger makes bad choices feel righteous. I paid for answers that cost me more than money. And in my rage, I didn't care.

And every single time I sought them out, Mikey got worse.

You'd think I would have seen the pattern, but the worse he got, the deeper my hatred for God grew. And I kept going back for more.

I cursed Him, along with the day I was born, and the date I married Larry. I even started to wonder if I'd have been better off childless, back in war-torn Bosnia. I shamefully confess it now, but that's where I was. Broken. Bitter. Done. None of it seemed to matter anyway. He wasn't listening.

Or maybe He was, and that was the worst part.

My Bible sat closed on the nightstand. Verses I once clung to with trembling hands now looked like nothing more than ink drained of meaning. Dust gathered on the cover until it spelled its own quiet verdict:

Silence.

But even silence has a breaking point.

Chapter 59

The Breaking Point

I *never meant to become the reason my son questioned his healing. But I was.*

After one session in particular, Mikey spiraled. I screamed, sheer panic. I called God a name I'll never repeat.

Not because I've forgotten it, but because I remember it too well.

And then—I felt it. A holy anger rose like a tidal wave, lifting me while my feet still clung to the earth. It wasn't a voice. It was weight.

Holy.

Terrifying.

Divine fury pressed in until every breath trembled beneath it.

God was angry—and He made sure I *knew* it.

Minutes later, we were back in the ICU. The same sterile cage with the same indifferent faces. And I hated Him all over again.

Didn't He know what hospitals did to me?

Didn't He care that I had nothing left?

Mikey—groggy, barely conscious—turned those swollen, exhausted, heartbreakingly sad eyes toward me.

"Mom… how will I ever get healed if you hate God?"

I froze.

Not because I had an answer, but because I didn't.

I wanted to tell him: "You will be healed, no matter what I believe."

Or, "It's okay. I'll carry you, even if I can't carry my faith."

But something in his words—raw, childlike, heartbreakingly pure—cracked the wall I'd built around my spirit.

I realized: I hadn't just walked away from God. I had tried to take Mikey with me. And if I couldn't find my way back, what would that mean for *him*?

That night, I didn't fall to my knees or open a Bible. I didn't even pray. But I whispered—to the dark, to the ceiling, to whatever God was left: "I don't forgive You yet…but please…don't walk away from *him* because of *me*."

That was the first time in months I stopped hating God long enough to ask Him for something other than justice. Not for me.

For my son.

Life (not) Worth Living

I remember texting the priest once: "I haven't slept in days. I think I lost my mind. ALL I can think about is ending this nightmare, once and for all. I just can't take it anymore!"

His response?!? "You can and you WILL. People who kill themselves are cowards, and cowards don't get to birth and raise someone like Mikey."

I stared at the words. They weren't cruel, but they missed the point. I didn't need correction. I needed a hand to hold the blade away from my heart.

And as if he could read my thoughts, he texted: "Bear the

cross you've been entrusted with without grunting. I pray for you all, daily."

His words landed like stones—true maybe, but useless to the drowning. *I see your prayers are working. Father!*

But the idea just wouldn't go away. As a matter of fact, it kept getting louder. More persuasive.

And then came the day.

The Day I Almost Did It

I was at work, barely holding it together. Larry kept texting, saying Mikey was having seizures again. He was exhausted. Said *he* couldn't take it anymore.

I stared at the screen and thought: *No more. I just can't take it anymore. Hell cannot be worse than this. This might be the day.* Two more patients to see, then it will all be over.

For good.

But something—some faint, flickering instinct—nudged me to text my curly-haired friend from Bible study:

"I don't know what's happening. I'm having thoughts of doing something really stupid. This is unbearable."

That message—that fragile string of words—was the lifeline God threw before I went under.

It kept me alive long enough for morning to find me.

Chapter 60

You Can't Lose What You Never Owned

T*hey say you can't lose what you never owned. Cute. Anyone who's spent nights in ER hallways knows better.*

Apparently, I didn't "own" faith.

I lost it, slowly. A prayer unanswered here, a prescription that made him worse there. Then it was wave after wave, pounding before I'd even surfaced from the last one. I thought I was stubborn enough to muscle through.

Spoiler: stubborn doesn't heal your child.

It doesn't change bloodwork. It does nothing for a sixteen-year-old begging you to understand and help him:

"*Mom, they're killing me.*"

Hardship doesn't care how tough you are, it peels you raw anyway.

When I finally admitted my faith was gone, I laughed.

"Well done," I told myself. "You've lost something you apparently never owned."

That's like losing your neighbor's lawnmower before you even borrowed it. Pure talent.

But the truth was, *I* chose to abandon God.

I shoved my faith away because trusting Him felt like the bigger lie. Better to cross my arms in rebellion than clasp them together one more time into that silence.

And getting it back?

It wasn't your fairy tale ending.

I found what I had thrown away the hard way—by crawling hospital corridors, by sleeping upright in plastic chairs. By testing it like a mechanic banging on a junk car:

"Does this thing even run?"

Sometimes it did. Sometimes it coughed smoke.

But at least I knew it was mine this time.

So yeah—maybe you can't lose what you never owned. But whatever I had, it was scraped together with duct tape and a string.

Just enough to get me through the next breath.

And somehow…

It was already waiting on the stairs.

I just didn't expect it to have a face.

Chapter 61

The Woman on the Stairs

I *was out of prayers. She showed up full of them.*

When I walked my next patient out, I saw her—uninvited, sitting on the stairs outside my office on a blistering Florida afternoon. Waiting. Not the friend I had texted, but the co-leader of our Bible study group. I rolled my eyes inside. *Seriously?*

She stood and hugged me. I hugged her back, but only out of habit.

"How are you?" she asked.

"Busy," I muttered. "*Why* are you here?"

She smiled. "I'm here. Praying for you. I love you."

The nerve. Didn't she know my God had let me down? Didn't she know I had other plans that day?

I hoped she'd leave. I *needed* her to leave. But when I walked out my last patient, she was still there. Smiling. Waiting.

"You and I need to talk," she said.

I didn't see what she had sacrificed, the love in her sweat, her presence and her persistence. All I saw was someone standing between me and the peace I thought death might finally give me.

She held me and prayed, but I kept looking at my phone, kept looking away. I kept hoping she'd just give up and *leave* already. But she didn't.

She said she wouldn't leave unless I promised not to do anything stupid.

So, I said, "I promise."

I lied.

The God Between Us

Mikey still believed in the God I had grown to resent. He kept asking me to do morning devotionals with him—like we used to—while I sat in the ruins of a faith I no longer recognized. His persistence didn't melt me: it grated. I was annoyed—not with him, *never* with him—but with what his questions represented. I was so far from God that the gesture felt like salt in an open wound.

Mikey didn't know I was bleeding faith he thought I still had. My boy just missed something we had once shared—something that, to him, still felt like comfort.

"Mom, will you do devotions with me?" He kept asking, with so much love and hope, but each time, I bristled even more. My answers came from the same place every time; exhausted, distant, honest in a way that probably sounded cold.

"Mikey… *you* stay close to God, please. Let me wrestle with this. This is part of *my* journey, and I need to be with it."

He nodded, then looked up at me—searching.

"But Mom, aren't we part of the same journey?"

Chapter 62

Between Two Worlds

They say cats have nine lives. I've come to believe that maybe, just maybe, we do too—only we lose a little more of ourselves each time we die while still breathing.

March 12, 2024.

A date I wish I could forget, but it lives in my bones now. The day Mikey went into status epilepticus. Again.

Another 911 call.

Another panicked ambulance ride to the infamous Coastal Bay ER—a place we trusted least but ended up in most.

I rode in the back, gripping Mikey's hand, whispering prayers I wasn't sure God even cared about anymore. We gave Mikey everything we could; rescue meds, nasal sprays. IVs in the ambulance.

Nothing was helping.

Tell Nadia I Love Her

Sirens screamed above us. The world outside smeared into a blur of red and white. Fear crawled up my throat and refused to leave.

I held on because letting go felt like betrayal.

Then… stillness. Not long, but long enough to terrify me.

His eyes opened and found mine, then, quiet as breath:

"Tell Nadia I only ever loved her."

Time broke.

He looked so unbearably sad, standing on the shoreline of two worlds, waiting for the tide to choose.

I wanted to tell him the truth. God, I wanted to. But *how* do you tell a boy clinging to life that the girl he saved his heart for never once reached back?

That she was living her life—carefree, driving now, dating now—without sending him a single word?

Not a single message.

How do you hand someone that kind of pain when they're already drowning, but still choosing love?

You don't.

You choose mercy instead.

So, I nodded.

What else can you do when a boy's last words hold someone else's name?

I squeezed his hand and let him believe she might still remember.

Chapter 63

The Life-Saving Call

I*n a room full of experts, it was a phone call that saved his life.*

The doors blew open and the light came crashing in.

At the ER, they moved quickly, calling code status before my heart took another beat.

"Mama, I know something bad is about to happen…"

"We've got him," a nurse said, but I didn't believe her.

He seized every thirty to forty seconds.

His beautiful brain couldn't rest. His organs were in danger. His heart was strained. The same lungs that once fought for their first breath now forgot how to take another.

The patient in the next room coughed and farted. Mikey kept seizing.

Shift change came. No one rushed anymore.

Mikey was left for dead.

And thank God—the very God I'd cursed just the day before—that I still had Dr. Walter's number. A local neurologist, a friend. I caught him right before his tennis match, gasping through tears, choking out the words: "Mikey is dying."

He didn't hesitate. "Hang up," he said. "I'm calling a friend in the ICU."

That call saved my son's life.

His colleague ran straight from the ICU to the ER and intubated Mikey on the spot, placing him in a medically induced *coma*. His body lay still. Eyes shut. A machine breathing for him. And even in a coma, he was still seizing. They told us he was alive, but unreachable.

Good Night, Moon

They moved him to the ICU room, and that's where the waiting began: slow, suffocating, relentless.

The hoping. The praying. The dying inside.

At some point I stepped into the hallway, trading one set of alarms for another. A man walked past me, furious, arguing on his phone about a parking ticket. I remember thinking that I would give anything to be that angry about something so small.

While I stood there, our world was already widening beyond those walls.

When word about Mikey's crises spread, the community answered the only way they knew how: by showing up. By holding vigils and praying in silence for Mikey's breath to return.

Jack came again.

A pastor I had never met entered quietly. He took Mikey's hand in one of his own, and mine in the other. He prayed as I wept into his hand, soaking his skin with my grief.

He left without a word.

We stayed.

Miriam spent the night with us in his room, offering her prayers as a light to help him find his way home.

~

Mikey was only three when he met Miriam, but some connections don't need time. Old souls recognize each other and build a family of their own.

One afternoon, he looked up at her in quiet wonder. "Ms. Miriam, *how* do you do that?"

"Do what, hunny bunny?"

"How do you make those beautiful lights come out of your hands?"

She didn't know what to say, but she knew—he was one of her own. A healer, though of what, none of us could say yet.

She was there for every birthday, every school play, every little moment Larry missed while he was deployed. She gave him books that made his imagination burn, and when she read to him—especially Goodnight Moon—he listened like her voice could hold the stars in place.

As she sat beside his bed, I prayed that the same light in her hands would find him again and pull him back from whatever darkness tried to take him.

Love like hers always finds its way—sometimes in a hand on your shoulder, sometimes in a voice that stays long after it's gone.

And sometimes… in a letter you forgot you wrote.

Chapter 64

Time in a Bottle

L*arry and I left Mikey's side only long enough to run home and shower. It was my turn to go.*

I told myself I only needed five minutes to feel human again. A shower. Clean clothes. A few breaths without alarms. But the house didn't feel like home without him in it. It felt paused.

I kicked off my shoes and went straight to the shower. The hot water helped my body. It did nothing for my mind. I grabbed a robe and walked down the hall, past the pile of mail I still couldn't face, into the bedroom. I sat on the edge of the bed, and my eyes drifted to the nightstand.

The drawer I almost never opened.

I stood to get dressed, but instead of heading toward the door, I turned back. My hand found the drawer without thinking. It stuck, like always. I eased it open and sat back hard, pressing a hand to my chest.

The time-capsule letter.

I wrote it to Mikey in 2014, when he turned ten and the world still made sense. It was a time when Band-Aids fixed almost anything, monsters lived only in storybooks, and questions were still small enough to answer with a kiss on the head or a made-up story at bedtime.

Long before the fear had a name and machines whispered what I was too afraid to say out loud.

A folded prayer, written to hold the things I hoped he'd carry into the life I thought he'd have time to live.

I didn't imagine I'd be slipping it under his pillow in the ICU, beside a tube taped to his mouth and a monitor that never stopped blinking, like it was trying to hold onto him for me. I left it there, just as I had written it.

Sometimes—right before the whole world tips—you get a moment so ordinary that you don't know it was holy until you're standing in its wreckage, aching for just five more seconds inside it.

Letter to My Son

February, 2014

To the awesomest son in the whole wide world.

I love you, Mikey, with every beat of my heart—more than sunshine, more than stars, more than every silly voice I ever used to make you laugh when you were sad.

Remember pancake Saturdays and your superhero cape. Remember the way we used to dance barefoot in the kitchen and how we made up new rules for Monopoly just so you'd win.

You are the most amazing person I've ever known. I didn't understand God until I saw His kindness written all over your face. Stay close to Him, baby—not because life is easy, but because it won't be.

Be gentle with people, especially the ones who seem hardest to love. They need it most.

Love wide open, but guard your heart like it's treasure—because it is.

Tell the truth, even when it trembles in your throat. Especially then.

Say "I'm sorry" like you mean it, and "I forgive you" like you really do.

Leave people better than you found them.

Be a good dad. Your children will learn who to become by watching YOU 🩶

And Mikey—stay curious. Ask "why" until your last breath. Never stop learning. Never stop wondering.

Never stop being—you.

Be grateful. Tithe 10, save 25, stretch out the rest. And when you fall, remember—the master is simply the beginner who kept getting back up.

I hope you always believe in yourself the way I believe in you. And if the world ever tries to convince you you're not enough—read this again.

I hope you never forget how deeply, wildly, and forever you are loved.

You are my heart, walking around in the world.

I live for you, Mikey. I always will.

Love,

Mama 🩶

Chapter 65

Machines Vs. The Divine

I once believed I was the one leading him. From the second Mikey arrived, he was already guiding me somewhere I could not yet see. I realized what he had been trying to show me only after the moment had passed beyond saving.

Off Key

Machines took turns pretending to be his lungs, his heart. The monitors flickered. The ventilator hissed. Each sound a reminder that his body was here, but *he* was not. None of them said the one thing I needed to hear.

All I could do was sit there, pretending not to fall apart.

I rubbed his swollen hands and feet. I bent his stiff joints.

I kept singing, knowing what singing meant to him. I begged him to blink. To squeeze my hand if he heard me. To come back.

Nothing.

Then, out of desperation, I tried humor—threatened that if he didn't blink, I would sing off key.

Nothing.

Then I did.

Still nothing.

My boy was somewhere far, far away.

Eventually, the nurses asked me to step out so they could change the sheets.

"We'll come get you," they said gently.

They pointed toward the family room—a sad, crowded space and the mindless flicker of a TV—but I just kept walking.

I wandered the hall like a phantom.

That's when I found it: a tiny hospital chapel. Empty. Still.

Holy.

Chapter 66

The Chapel

I *knelt before an open Bible I couldn't even read, begging a God I wasn't sure was even listening.*

Inside, a small altar held an open Bible. A manual for the desperate. For the lost. For the mother begging God to trade her life for her child's. Above the altar, a round stained-glass window of praying hands, surrounded by bright flowers.

I knelt and pressed my face into the open Bible (written in Spanish)—familiar in spirit, but unreadable to me in that language. The faith was mine, but in that moment, it felt distant.

I felt distant.

A stranger in this place, in this country, and—God help me—a stranger to God.

My sorrow soaked the thin, crinkled pages of scripture. I broke down and sobbed until my bones hurt. I bargained with a deaf God with everything I had:

"Please… Not him. Take *me* instead, this is all *my* fault. Save *him*."

I wept until the well inside me ran dry. My knees throbbed

from the hard floor. Eventually, I sat back, my head resting against the table leg that held the Bible—as if it were holding me.

I don't know how long I stayed there, only that the pain slowly gave way to numbness.

~

Before I even looked up, I knew I wasn't alone anymore. "Uncle Jack" (as Mikey calls him) stood there, his face tight with worry and a knowing he couldn't hide. He knelt beside me, pulled me into his arms, and wept with me.

For a long time, neither of us moved.

When he finally spoke, it felt as if the words had been waiting years for this moment.

"Gordana… there's something I never told you."

My throat was raw. I didn't trust my voice. I just nodded.

"Years ago," he said, "I used to wonder where the spirit goes when we sleep. I thought maybe… part of us leaves for a while. Fighting things we can't see. Keeping the darkness at bay."

He let out a shaky breath.

"I never told anyone that. They would have thought I was losing my mind."

He paused.

"When I look back now, I can't help but wonder if I was already discerning your son."

He let the words settle.

"Michael Gabriel," he said quietly. "The warrior and the messenger."

Another pause.

"I don't think that's random. I don't think any of this is."

He kept his eyes on the pages in front of us.

"I think that in those frightening moments when he seems gone, he's fighting where he's needed—somewhere we can't follow, in ways we can't see, doing work we don't yet understand… even when it breaks us to watch."

This was a friend reaching for language big enough to hold pain without collapsing under it.

"You're not losing him, Gordana," he said. "And you're not alone in this fight. Not for one second."

His quiet strength steadied me, lifted me, and walked me back down that corridor, back to where death was closing in around my boy.

In the ICU, Mikey remained lifeless. Larry arrived not long after. Together, we rallied everyone we knew to pray.

Long seconds bled into minutes. Minutes into hours. Hours into days.

Days collapsed into endless nights… bringing nothing but sorrow.

They all stretched into a full week.

Still, nothing changed.

Chapter 67

Come From the Four Winds

T*hey told me the machines would be turned off. I wasn't ready to say goodbye.*

March 17, 2024. St. Augustine

A pair of rubber-soled shoes squeaked on the tile. The doctor stepped in, clipboard clutched tight to his chest. The overhead lights buzzed behind his head like flies. His strong accent scraped against the edges of my memory, but I didn't have time to remember from where.

"I'm sorry," he said, his voice too steady for what he was about to say. "We have to take him off life support."

I stared at him, stupid with shock.

"His vitals are unstable. His brain isn't sustaining autonomic function. The machines are keeping him breathing, but not for long. We need to know… now."

He looked at me the way doctors look at families in TV shows. "Pray he breathes on his own."

Pray…

Like it was that easy. Like I hadn't already emptied every

prayer out of my chest on the chapel floor, down to the marrow.

Now I was to see if the Earth would still let him stay. I nodded, but it was a surrender.

Larry and I forgot about the divorce. Our hands locked so tight it hurt, but letting go would've hurt worse.

The respiratory tech removed the tube.

Silence.

Machines beeped in time with nothing. The tech shifted, fidgeting now—glancing at the monitor, then at us, then back again.

It was too quiet. Too long. Too final.

Then—

A cough.

Then another, like something was clawing its way back through him. I didn't realize I was whispering until I heard my own voice break: *"Come from the four winds… Come, breath."*

He gasped.

Then took a breath. *His* breath.

God gave it back. He was breathing on his own!

The moment breath filled his lungs, my hands came together in a shaky, stunned applause… like my body was celebrating what my heart couldn't yet believe.

Around us, relief broke like dawn: nurses grinned through tears, monitors steadied, someone whispered *Thank You.*

For a breathless second the whole room felt weightless, suspended between heaven and Earth.

Mikey's eyes fluttered open.

Chapter 68

My Friend, J.C.

H*e left this world. Then he was sent back.*

When Mikey opened his eyes, it wasn't just breath that returned to him.

It was light.

A glow seemed to cling to him, faint but unmistakable, as if heaven refused to let go completely. His body shuddered, and his fingers curled weakly against the blanket, but there was peace in his face… a peace I hadn't seen in months.

"Mama… Dad…" His voice was thin, but sure. "I saw Jesus. I saw Jesus! Thank You, God…" He closed his eyes and whispered, "Thank You for saving my life."

We lifted him gently, our hands trembling more than his. He felt lighter—too light—like part of him was still in the hands of the One who held him when we could not.

"I saw the light," he whispered.

Everything in the room froze. Even the monitors seemed to quiet themselves.

"I was with Jesus. I wept for Him. And He… He wept for *me*."

His eyes were glassy, looking somewhere past us—through the wall, maybe beyond the world itself. His words fell like stones into water, creating ripples that shook everything I believed.

"He showed me things I don't know how to explain. Stars, floating like music. People—people I didn't even know—praying for me. And angels. I saw angels fall trying to keep me alive."

His hands trembled in his lap. There were IV lines threaded through his veins, but he clutched at them like they were strings pulling him back down from heaven.

"And the music," he said, voice gone soft. "It was the most beautiful thing I've *ever* heard."

He tried to laugh, but it caught in his chest. He looked at me with that crooked little smile that used to mean he wanted a cookie before dinner.

"I'm sure it wasn't *your* singing," he teased weakly.

Something inside me broke and healed all at once. Even now, fresh from the edge of eternity, he was comforting *me.*

I managed a grin. "Oh, trust me! I sang off-key on purpose, to annoy you just enough that you'd come back and tease me."

His smile faltered, then the truth broke through.

"I didn't want to come back," he whispered. Tears gathered, shimmering like something holy. "I told Jesus that. I felt free. No pain. No fear. No seizures. I was safe. I was loved… more deeply than I've ever felt on earth."

I felt the breath drain from my lungs.

My child had tasted heaven.

He took another breath, then turned to look at me—really look at me—and everything in his face changed.

"But He told me…" Mikey's lips quivered. "He said, 'It's not your time yet.'"

Silence pressed in around us, thick as a blanket.

And then, as if the universe wanted to remind me we were still on hospital time, a nurse poked her head in the door, completely unaware she'd walked into a moment that had just rearranged my entire soul.

"Hi there," she said, cheerful. "Anyone need juice?"

Mikey blinked at her. "I just came back from heaven."

She nodded with the polite glaze of someone used to hearing strange things from patients.

"Okay… so… orange or apple?"

Then realized from all our faces that she'd misread the room.

"I'll… uh… come back later," she murmured, retreating.

Her footsteps faded away down the hall, and the room slowly remembered what silence felt like.

After a long moment, Mikey spoke again, barely above a breath.

"Mama… why were you crying in the chapel?"

My heart *seized.*

My son—while caught between this life and the next—had seen me.

Kneeling on the cold chapel floor.

Crying.

Begging a God I wasn't even sure would hear me. Breaking in front of the altar.

And somehow—*somehow*—he came back.

Chapter 69

God Loved Him First

The machines steadied his body. Grace steadied mine. For the first time in months, I didn't fight it. I finally let God in.

I didn't plan on crawling back to Him that day.

The week before, the month before, even the night before, I had shelved faith like an old book—still mine, just pushed up high and covered in dust. I hadn't stopped believing, but belief felt far away, like a song I used to know by heart but hadn't sung in years.

But then, March 12.

It wasn't my experience that changed everything.

It was Mikey's.

I know how that sounds. People hear it and hesitate. Some nod politely; others step back, unsure what to make of it. But none of that mattered, because when Mikey spoke, there was no hesitation in him. Just a certainty that landed hard and true inside me.

I remember looking at him—really looking—and something was different. Not in his features, but in his presence. His eyes. His *peace*. It wasn't imagined, and it certainly wasn't a wishful thinking.

It was real. As real as the sun rising without our permission.

God loved him first.

On my best day, even when I gave Mikey every part of me, my love could *never* match His. And instead of that breaking me, it broke something *in* me: the illusion that Mikey was mine to keep.

And that truth set me free.

I (wrongly) assumed my job was to protect him. That if I stayed strong, stayed good, stayed in control—God would see that, and spare him.

But Mikey didn't need me to be God. He already had Him.

And in calling Mikey, God was calling me, too.

I felt it rising in me, like something I'd swallowed years ago had finally made its way back up:

The grief I'd buried in meal plans and prescriptions.

The control I'd used to outrun fear.

The ache I'd numbed with information and medical jargon. It all rose at once–and I let it.

I dropped to my knees beside his bed and whispered the words I hadn't dared pray in years: "*Your* will, not mine, be done."

The words of a daughter finally coming home.

But let me be honest: coming home didn't erase the pain or silenced the questions.

One question that haunted me then—and still knocks on my chest when the world gets quiet—is this:

Did my son have to die so I'd come back to God?

I don't know.

Maybe it was never mine to know.

Maybe the not knowing is its own kind of mercy.

Chapter 70

The Song in His Soul

Long before I knew where life would take him, music was already leading him home. One day strangers would step between us, deciding when—and if—I was allowed to hear it.

The Unsung Life of a Lion

Mikey always carried a song in his breath:

He sang when he played.

He sang when he cleaned his room—dramatic, off-key, and entirely on purpose.

He even sang when he brushed his teeth, though I had to remind him more than once not to spit to the beat of the music.

He joined the youth chorus at fourteen without hesitation, walking in like he already knew the music. That same director teaches him now, years later, in the adult chorus. Still believing in that voice that wavers, cracks, forgets its place… but always finds its way home again.

Every Wednesday, they work together: scales, breathing, posture, patience. Brick by brick, rebuilding what illness tried to steal. One note at a time. A thread he could still follow, even when everything else felt out of tune.

Music remained the medicine his brain used to remember what it once knew by heart.

"Mr. Mike" knew that.

That's why he never gave up, even on the hard days when Mikey could barely lift his head, when medication fogged his mind and his voice struggled to hold a pitch.

Mikey kept showing up.

Mr. Mike kept reminding him: breathe from the diaphragm, focus on tone, let the sound carry through the pain.

One rehearsal began like all the others, until Mikey's tonic seizure broke through the music, sounding like a night terror. And to many in the room, that's exactly what it felt like. Faces froze, glances shifted, and a few people looked away, caught between worry and not knowing what to do.

Before I could move, Mr. Mike stepped forward—calm as breath—and said:

"He's fine. Let's give him a minute. The music doesn't stop for courage."

And just like that, he silenced every whisper and every fear.

A quiet reminder that music and mercy often sound the same.

"Mr. Mike" still teases him. Still expecting the best, correcting him, pushing him—"Louder, Mikey. Hold it longer."

And somehow, he still makes us laugh.

One concert lives in my memory like it happened five minutes ago.

The boys' choir had just begun *"In the jungle, the mighty jungle, the lion sleeps tonight."* From the front row, I whispered, "Go on, Mikey—wake the lion."

He grinned, rolled his eyes like any fourteen-year-old

would, and sang like he owned the jungle—until his voice cracked halfway through the high note.

The look on his face?

Half horror, half amusement. Stuck between boyhood and whatever came next. The audience chuckled, warm and kind.

After the concert, Mr. Mike didn't miss a beat. He called out from the stage: "It's all right, Mikey! Every lion's roar squeaks before it soars!"

Everyone laughed. Mikey laughed too, shaking his head like he was deciding whether to be embarrassed or proud.

After the show, I teased him: "So... are you the lion or the lullaby?"

He grinned and shrugged. "Depends who's listening, Mama."

And now…

now I can't hear that song without wishing my lion would roar again.

Mikey made the hard parts of life worth living. He could look at you at 6:42 AM—sleep still clinging to his lashes—and smile like he was seeing you for the very first time. Every morning, without fail, he'd wake, blink once, then smile like sunrise—and plant a kiss on my cheek like it was his favorite part of the day.

He didn't wait for joy. He brought it.

He didn't just *sing* music. He *was* music.

One morning, the music didn't come.

Chapter 71

Crisis After Crisis

W*hen the music left Mikey, it didn't slam the door on its way out. It slipped out like it knew where it was going, and I was the only one still chasing the sound.*

The silence didn't pass. It settled in.

What should've been a bad day became a season.

From April through August, crisis was the only language we spoke.

Hospitals replaced calendars, time marked only by shifts and prayers. They took pieces of who we were when this all began. By July, Mikey was intubated again. Another coma. Another round of desperate prayers scraping raw against Heaven's gates. The hospital lights blinded like interrogation lamps, and every beep was another reminder that my boy's life dangled between wires and willpower.

A nurse knew my name by now. She laid her hand on my shoulder.

"He's strong," she said softly.

I stared at her hand for a long moment, imagining it in a Batman glove.

This was the same nurse who had laughed with Mikey a

few years back in this very hospital. He was younger then, still joking with her even with IVs in his arms:

Me: "I know that look a little too well. Spit it out—what are you up to this time?"

Mikey: "Nothing. Just thinking about swapping all the nurses' scrubs for superhero costumes. Imagine Batman taking your blood pressure."

Me: "That's not medicine, that's Comic-Con."

Mikey: "Same difference. Both save lives."

The memory flashed and cracked like a photograph burning at the edges. Tears betrayed me again.

She said: "He's got this. He *is* a superhero."

I looked up and whispered, "He's twenty. He shouldn't have to be."

By August, I couldn't remember the last time I slept through the night. Too many ICU doors had whispered shut behind me, carrying conversations I wasn't meant to hear. Too many white coats offering hope with one hand and stripping it away with the other.

Exhaustion had tunneled past bone, so deep I began to wonder:

How much can a human heart endure before it simply forgets how to beat?

And still… love wouldn't let me stop.

If my boy could find a breath, then so could I.

I kept breathing.

That's how I kept fighting.

Chapter 72

Wars and Battlefields

Truth is, the battlefield wasn't confined to the ICU. It followed us home. An uninvited guest that slept at the foot of our bed.

No one sees the hours spent arguing with insurance, or claps when you learn oxygen flow rates at 2 a.m. There's no medal for memorizing drug schedules or for smiling at doctors while you're breaking inside. But you do it. Every day. Because love, in crisis, looks a lot like endurance.

Survival had replaced intimacy. The logistics of keeping a child alive left no room for the language of marriage.

We still moved around each other. Passed coffee mugs. Folded laundry. Took turns in hospital chairs. If his hand brushed mine, it was by accident now.

One night, as we crossed paths in the hallway—both half-awake, half-undone—he asked quietly, "Did you refill his meds?"

"I think so," I whispered.

We both paused, staring at the floor like it held the answer.

"I'll check again," he said.

And that counted as connection.

The version of us that once shared glances across crowded rooms? That laughed over late-night pancakes?

That version had gone quiet, too.

Two soldiers in the same war, fighting on different fronts. The person you love can become the one you forget to grieve with simply because they're still standing beside you. And you keep promising yourselves you'll come back to each other.

Later. When things calm down. When he's better.

But time was always the one thing slipping through our hands. We were learning to survive a war with no medals, no map, and no guarantee the people we loved would still be standing when it ended.

And the scariest part?

Sometimes, the ones we lost weren't in hospital beds.

Sometimes, they were in the mirror.

Bottomless Bottle

Larry leaned across the table with that cocky grin.

"I'm just warning you," he said. "Back in college, they called me The Paddle."

I twirled my paddle like I'd been born with it.

"Cute," I said. "In kindergarten they called me The Champ. So… good luck, Paddle."

I served. He didn't even touch the ball.

"Okay, Forrest," he laughed. "You're supposed to flirt when you're dating, not crush my spirit."

"This *is* flirting, Mr. Chocolate Pants."

"I think I just fell for a monster."

"You're welcome."

Somewhere along the way, the table cracked, and the laughter started echoing instead of landing. One afternoon, I walked in from work and smelled it before I saw him—the sharp, yeasty scent that never hides well.

I asked. He denied.

I kept listening to a man who wanted me to forget I could still smell the truth.

He stared at me; I stared back.

He wandered into the garage, pretending to shred old boxes: distraction disguised as productivity. I followed, not to accuse, but to be near enough to see. Something made me flip the recycling bin. Four bottles rolled out—wet, sour, undeniable. His eyes said what he wouldn't: he'd already lost more than he could fix. I held up the bottles like a verdict, waiting for him to meet my eyes.

"These aren't mine," he said, steady as a lie rehearsed too many times.

I shook my head. "You think I don't know the smell of heartbreak by now?"

Part of me wanted to hand him an Oscar. The rest of me wanted to hand him a mirror.

And right there—beer in hand, lies between us—I saw all of him at once:

The man I fell in love with.

The man I was losing.

And the impossible space in between.

Then from inside, Mikey called out. We froze. Whatever battle was happening between us would have to wait.

We ran inside.

Side by side—not together, but in the same direction.

Chapter 73

Choosing to Stay When I Could Leave

M*arriage didn't fail us. Crisis did. And some days, I hated that I couldn't tell the difference.*

I've stood at the edge of our marriage more times than I'll ever admit. Moments where leaving felt cleaner than staying, where the fantasy of escape looked like peace. But I didn't go. I stayed because even in the worst of it, there was still something in him that reached for something in me.

And that something mattered.

He loved me and Mikey the best he knew, but his love came shaped by the things that had broken him. He tried. God knows he tried.

No one teaches soldiers how to come home and be husbands.

I married a man who could walk through a battlefield without blinking but nearly came undone in a hospital room when our son stopped breathing.

And in those moments, it was me who had to stay standing.

That's the part no one tells you about: when you marry a soldier, you'll become one.

~

We didn't have a perfect love story. We had daily fights. For presence. For healing. For faith. For a future that didn't resemble the past.

It's not pretty, but it's honest.

I didn't stay because I'm some kind of hero: something in me refused to believe the story had to end in failure.

Maybe that's faith.

Or maybe it's just that sometimes the bravest thing you can do is keep choosing a life that hasn't turned out the way you planned—and love the people in it anyway.

And so here we are:

One miracle child—still standing.

One weary mother—still praying.

One wounded soldier—still struggling.

And one faithful God—still not letting go.

Staying didn't make me weaker; it showed me how to kneel when I wanted to run.

Because the God who never left us in the hospital, in the courtroom, in the furnace—is the same God who never leaves a soldier behind.

Or his wife.

Chapter 74

The Valleys and The Mountains

T*he valleys broke me. The mountains didn't fix me. Yet in both, I learned to release the burden of needing answers.*

The mountains have always whispered peace to me, perhaps because they stand so still, unmoved by the storms that rage at their feet.

New wounds had been carved, old scars reopened. Different battles were behind us, and new ones still lay ahead.

War still raged, yet the ridges stood unchanged.

Twice in two years, Maggie Valley (North Carolina) called our names, and twice, I was reminded: You can't have peaks without valleys. You walk through both, or not at all.

We traded the noise of the world for the hush of wind through pine, and let the silence I'd once feared and mistaken for abandonment say what words no longer could.

And in that quiet, I realized: I wasn't the first to accuse God of silence. David did. Job did. Even Jesus—*My God, my God, why have You forsaken me?*

There's a strange comfort in that. Maybe God's silence

isn't absence, but space where faith learns to breathe without crutches or applause.

The mountains just stood there—ancient, unbothered, unbroken.

And somehow, that was answer enough.

Chapter 75

Hiking Toward Peace

I *used to say bravery and stubborn hope were twins born of the same impulse—to keep moving when everyone else froze.*

My father and I learned that in a war zone. Years later, Larry and I were learning it again on a different battlefield, chasing life wherever it dared to appear.

Maybe we were brave, maybe we were foolish, but we kept going—not to outrun the pain, but to remind ourselves that joy was still possible.

When Mikey felt even half-decent, we packed the car and traveled, sometimes across states, sometimes just across town. Each trip was a rebellion. The Smoky Mountains. The Grand Canyon.

Sedona's red breath of stone. And, of course, New York—not only for the *Harry Potter* play, but for its famous electric hum.

Every mile, a small act of defiance against despair.

I still laugh thinking about that double-decker tour in Manhattan.

We sat up top, the wind tangling Mikey's shaggy hair,

when a couple of tourists behind us joked that nothing good ever came out of New Jersey.

Mikey turned, grinning that sideways grin that always gave him away. "That's only, bro," he said, "because you never met Mr. Mike."

They laughed. I did too. We made new friends.

And for a split second—between illness and skyline—my son became both punchline and preacher: proof that light still talks back.

A few weeks before Mikey would brave the Ohio Hospital for more invasive testing, we packed the car and drove to the mountains—our dress rehearsal for courage.

We hiked the Smokies together, following trails that twisted like veins through the hills. Waterfalls thundered nearby, mist rising like incense from rock and river.

I watched Mikey breathe it in, steps sure on uneven ground.

At one point, we stopped beside a stream, its current tumbling over stones slick as glass.

Mikey kicked off his shoes and stepped in. The water was snowmelt-cold, clear enough to show every vein of quartz beneath his feet. He stood there, barefoot in the rush, head tipped back toward the light, sunlight breaking over him in fragments.

"This feels… good," he said, voice low, almost surprised. "Like my brain's not fighting me so hard here."

"Able to relax?" I asked.

He looked up, eyes half-closed against the glare. "Yeah," he said. "I feel… like me again."

Without a word, Larry and I slipped off our shoes and stepped in beside him. The shock of the cold climbed our legs, but none of us moved.

For a moment, the three of us just stood there—ankle-deep, the current threading around us—and it felt like the river itself was holding us upright.

Mikey's fragile strength carried us further than we thought we could go. Somewhere along the way, amid the cracks, Larry and I found flickers of togetherness.

And somehow, in the stillness between heartbreaks, we rediscovered what grief had tried to steal: that joy is not the absence of suffering, but the audacity to find light—and to love life exactly as it is.

Maybe real courage is not the charge into battle, but the quiet decision to keep waking up.

To pack the car and chase the sunset.

To laugh on the days that let you.

And to remember—always—that joy was never lost.

It was only waiting, ankle-deep in the water, eyes lifted to the light.

Chapter 76

The Cutting Edge of Hope

F*aith doesn't always ride in on miracles. Sometimes it crawls in—through grief, through surgery, through the sound of your son's voice on the phone when you can't touch his face.*

I stood in the kitchen, elbows pressed to the counter, forehead resting against the cold granite like a child who wanted out of the world. The tile beneath my bare feet was cold, damp in one spot where I'd spilled something earlier and forgotten to clean it up. The clock on the microwave glowed an uncaring green:

7:18 A.M.

I had just been on FaceTime with Mikey, right before they rolled him to the operating room. He looked groggy but brave, softness in his voice.

"You okay, Mama?" he asked, as if *I* were the one who needed protecting.

"I'm here," I told him. "I'm right here."

I wasn't there in body, or within reach, but here—where the weight lives.

At twenty-one, my son was signing a surgical consent,

saying "yes" to a very invasive brain surgery with more risks than the dreams he'd only just begun to build. At an age when most kids are signing apartment leases, internship offers, or wedding invitations, mine was signing away pieces of his own safety for a slightest chance at relief.

I could almost feel the pen etching itself across my heart.

My Mustache Man was in SEEG surgery. Skull drilled through, wires and electrodes placed in his beautiful brain. Seizures induced to locate the misfiring and brain monitored in real time.

Larry sat in the waiting room, watching the monitor board for updates—a man who had lost his military job eight months ago—had the time now, but not the stability.

He went with Mikey, because someone had to.

I stayed, because someone had to.

I had become the only provider, and the love letters stamped in red from hospital billing departments kept arriving, some marked "second notice," others "final warning."

I stayed because I have panic attacks in hospitals now.

Because trauma doesn't always stay where it happened.

So, we divided the load, not evenly, but faithfully.

Larry held our son's body.

I held everything else.

My phone buzzed. It was Larry.

I didn't even say hello. "You're in?" I asked.

"They took him back," he said, his voice already frayed. I could hear the background hum—the blur of the intercom, the beeping of machines. "He signed the papers. IV's in. He's prepped. They're moving him now."

"Is he nervous?" My voice cracked.

"He was," Larry replied. "Didn't show it. You know him."

I swallowed hard. "I should be there."

"He asked me to tell you that The Mustache Man loves you, right before they wheeled him in."

I nodded, even though he couldn't see me. "Tell him I love him, an infinity plus one."

"I already did. Once per minute, as instructed," he managed to tease.

The line went dead.

I set the phone down, face-up on the counter, and didn't move. It was like my body had fused to the kitchen tile, cemented to the last place I heard my son's name spoken out loud.

The microwave clock blinked: 07:36. He was in the OR now. And I was standing in a kitchen that smelled like nothing.

Another buzz: a text from Larry. *IV in. Prepping for anesthesia.*

I stared at the words until they blurred. The green dot next to his name pulsed like a heartbeat. My fingers shook as I typed: "Tell him I'm here."

No reply.

Another text followed: "He's in OR. They're starting."

I pressed both palms to the counter, trying to steady myself. My mug tipped, hot liquid splashing down my wrist. I didn't even flinch.

08:12. No updates.

08:47. Still nothing.

I kept refreshing the app. No updates.

I started wiping the same section of countertop over and over. Opened a drawer. Closed it. Opened it again. The house was so quiet it roared. Somewhere far off, a lawn mower sputtered to life. The silence between updates started to feel like a cliff edge.

At 10:14 A.M., it hit me like a fist: They're drilling now.

Somewhere in Ohio, beneath surgical lights too bright for

mercy, my Miracle Child lay sedated and pinned with wires. Somewhere, a neurosurgeon steadied his hand over a drill. One wrong movement, and Mikey could come back altered.

Or not come back at all.

I kept rubbing the bruise on my right arm from 2020 that never went away.

My mind flashed to his curls as a toddler and how they smelled of salt and sunscreen. His small hand in mine. His voice, reading Harry Potter spells out loud. All of it—soft, ordinary, holy—pressed up against the image of a drill piercing bone.

The hours muddled together. Oreo curled beneath the table like he knew better than to ask anything of me.

And then, without ceremony, the jagged and desperate cry came:

God… I can't be there, but You're already where I'm not.

Cover Michael with warmth in that cold room. Keep Larry strong and calm.

Give me just enough courage to keep breathing from here.

Please, let this be the moment everything changes.

For better, for once.

I wiped my eyes.

This was surgery, too, slicing through the soul and laying it bare on the altar of belief.

By the sixth hour, my phone was slick with sweat. The green clock read 1:44 P.M. The counter was spotless, my hands raw from scrubbing.

Finally, it vibrated.

Larry: "*Closing up now. He's stable. Still under.*"

I slid down the cabinet until I was sitting on the floor, knees pulled up, tile cold against my skin. My hands still shook.

I whispered two words, barely audible.

"Thank you."

Today, I stood at the cutting edge of hope, one foot in the past, one foot in the unknown.

And nothing but faith asking me to step forward.

Chapter 77

The Weight I Chose to Carry

T*he boys took a trip to Ohio.*
I took a guilt trip.

My "yes" came quietly, as a whispered agreement made in the corners of responsibility, a quiet nod to duty over desire. I agreed to stay behind—to save money, to be practical—while my child boarded a plane and flew away to face a hospital bed and a surgeon's blade.

I stayed behind while my son went forward.

And then? I ate grief three times a day. Washed it down with guilt.

I watched him on FaceTime: my son, my heart—his bones sharper than they should be, his cheeks hollowed by illness, his body dissolving into hospital linen like sand into the tide. My soul slid deeper into a place I thought I'd already bottomed out of.

There's always a deeper ache, isn't there?

It stayed with me through that surgery… and the brain bleed that followed. It remained in that cold hospital room, watching machines breathe assurance when doctors couldn't.

At least Larry was with him.

~

Fridays now haunt me.

The trauma lives where doctors disappear into long weekends, and decisions fall to residents with weary eyes and distracted hearts. I remember the way we were left behind, unheard and unseen so many times, while others barbecued and slept in.

And now, it was happening again.

Another Friday was approaching.

I looked at the bruise on my arm again.

With some supernatural strength, I found ways to remember all the good things… remind myself that, against all odds, we still live in the middle of someone else's miracle.

So… tell me, how is *your* day so far?

The job you dread? Someone else would give anything for it.

The child who exhausts you? Someone else is staring at an empty crib.

The messy kitchen? The loud house? The unending list of chores?

They are all signs of life. Of normal.

Of blessings.

So, count them. Count the crumbs, the car rides, the arguments, the laughter. Count the clean water, the working limbs, the taste of food, the silence of peace.

As for me, I'm here… sitting with *my* guilt like an old, unwelcome friend. But I'm also counting my blessings. Even now. *Especially* now.

I signed up for this. And I'd sign up again.

Because love does that; it carries the unbearable weight and walks into fire it didn't start.

Because anything we have today… we might long for tomorrow.

And if your Sundays are filled with lightness and laughter, know this—they only exist because of The Friday.

Chapter 78

MARVELous Mom

I *FINALLY SLEPT 8 HOURS!!!*

The whole week combined since the boys left for Ohio, but, whatever.

July 2025. Day 7 in Ohio

Seven days deep in this void of loneliness, and my soul was still at the airport—frozen in the moment, watching them walk away toward the departing gate, toward the hospital, toward uncertainty. My feet were planted, but my heart left with them.

I ached, because a mother isn't meant to be separated from her child. Or escorted by security from an infamous hospital we no longer talk about. Especially since and because of that.

On one of our calls, Mikey said he'd been watching Marvel movies on hospital TV channels. And instantly, my heart time-traveled to our old living room, lit up with the colorful chaos of Marvel heroes—Iron Man soaring, Spider-Man flipping through cityscapes, Captain America throwing his shield with righteous strength… my boyfriend Thor. Black Panther.

But the biggest hero of them all sat right beside me, wrapped in a blanket, holding my hand, eyes wide and sparkling with wonder. And then he'd turn to me, press his warm cheek against mine, and say with all the certainty of a child's heart:

"Mama," he whispered once, melting my heart, "You're my MARVELous MOM."

He couldn't quite pronounce it, and I didn't want to correct it. I wouldn't have changed a single syllable, because, in his voice, I heard something divine. In his eyes, I saw strength I didn't know I had. And in that moment, I believed I could move mountains or melt iron. Lift a truck or fly through fire.

Because in his eyes, I was a superhero.

We laughed together. We had superhero adventures of our own—pillow fights and popcorn, plastic Tupperware shields and wooden spoon swords.

A decade later, my child's words would echo louder and deeper, long after the costumes were put away.

The real villains came, and I was not wearing a cape.

Every time he laughed after a night full of tears… every time he pushed through his exhaustion… every time he got back up and tried again—he showed me something I needed to see: Not all heroes wear capes, and not all moms feel MARVELous.

Grace has a way of making warriors out of the weary.

And me?

Here I stand—still tired, sometimes trembling, but unshaken, because I am still *his* MARVELous Mom.

I'm not perfect, but I am chosen, and God equips the called.

I was learning that one bent knee at a time.

Chapter 79

Bee Gees and Bent Knees

T*ime was mine, but peace wasn't. I could close my eyes whenever I wanted—sleep just didn't want me back.*

Ohio Hospital. 14,657 recorded seizures.

Even from states away, I felt his suffering long before the machines ever did. It wasn't the worst thing a parent could face, but it was far more than I knew how to carry.

That's the truth of it.

The deepest kind of defeat is realizing just how powerless we really are.

With every mile, every new zip code, the story felt like it was walking itself down a dark staircase no child should ever be dragged into… and no mother should ever have to follow behind.

I knelt in a place that felt too small for the weight of my heart, dreading the next text.

I was reaching for a straw—any scrap of memory, any glimpse of Mikey as his goofy, healthy self.

"Mom, not everything needs a soundtrack"—usually right before busting a move to one!

Then I found that video… Tall. Curly. Happy. Peach fuzz soft under his nose. My boy—healthy and handsome—a ninth grader on the gym floor, dancing his cute butt off and lip-syncing to *Staying Alive.*

I broke fully, loudly, terribly. Sobs that I could swear didn't even belong to me.

Because that song…

I remembered doing CPR on him in 2019, matching my compressions to that exact beat while waiting for the ambulance. My hands doing what his heart couldn't. Traitor tears, again.

"Staying Alive" doesn't mean what it used to.

"God… is this the end of the road?

If it is, just tell me. Tell me so I can love him even more, if that's even possible. Are we ever truly ready to let go?"

I didn't know what lesson I was supposed to be learning in this unbearable sifting, only what I was begging for:

Let me see him dance again.

Let me see him living, not just surviving.

Let him be surrounded by laughter, mischief, and music.

Let him be.

That morning, I tried to pray and couldn't form a single word. I just dropped to my bent knees—again—and whispered through tears:

"Good morning. Guess who… again."

One tear, then another. One sob, then another. My hand reached out as if I could touch the memory in that video, as if my fingers could smooth his curls or trace the smile I missed so much. My journal pages soaked through.

My knees ached under the weight of it all.

My heart ached more.

And when I had nothing left—no words, no strength—I just said:

"Amen."

Chapter 80

Power Made Perfect in Weakness

I *thought weakness was a flaw, a sign I wasn't praying enough, trusting enough, doing enough, or being strong enough. I kept asking myself the same question: Was I enough?*

I thought if I just had more faith, I'd be able to stand tall(er)—unshaken, unwavering—but the shaking came anyway; the floor split open, the walls trembled, my knees buckled.

And I fell! Not once or gracefully, but repeatedly. And hard.

There were nights I sat in cold hospital rooms, watching beeping monitors instead of stars, wondering how many people had been helped there… and how many hadn't.

I was anxiously waiting for Larry's update, wondering why the second surgery was taking so long… The house was silent, but my mother-heart was anything but.

Just a few more days until I would lay these puffy eyes on my lonely only. And with his return would come that strange blend of joy and weakness, because I've learned to live between celebration and fear, between the "yes" and the "not-yet."

I no longer had to hold it all together.

Chapter 81

The Bleeding Heart. And Brain.

kiss to build a dream on.

August, 2025. The Day Mikey Returned From Ohio

Oreo knew before I did.

Twenty minutes before it was time to leave, he started pacing by the door—tail up, ears alert, eyes locked on the driveway like it owed him something. He knew that airport run by scent alone.

I wore the effort of someone who hadn't given up. I even fixed my hair, trying to convince the mirror to believe in hope with me.

The drive was quiet. Oreo shifted between the front seat and the back window, smudging the glass with nose prints that felt like fingerprints from a better year.

I could barely contain myself. My heart was thudding out seconds like a countdown, one beat closer to seeing Mikey again, to wrapping my arms around him, kissing his forehead, maybe even pulling his finger just to make him groan and say, "Mom, *seriously*!"

I would've taken anything. A smirk. An eye-roll. That half-smile that meant he was still in there somewhere. When we pulled up to the terminal, Oreo nearly clawed his way out the window. His whining was so loud I had to remind him—and myself—to breathe.

The doors slid open.

I spotted Larry first, but Mikey's shoulder was not next to his. When my eyes lowered, I realized he was pushing the wheelchair, slowly, like they'd practiced the exit. And in it—my Mustache Man.

Paler, thinner. Hoodie up, head low. But alive. Here.

Oreo ran to him like we'd rehearsed this reunion for years.

Mikey didn't respond with a laugh, or a "Hey, buddy." He barely moved.

I rushed toward him, tears already threatening to spill, arms open, ready to fold him in like it would erase the weeks we'd lost.

He didn't reach back.

I leaned in to kiss him, and he turned his head slightly, eyes not meeting mine, just... gone.

"Later," he said.

It was the first time in his entire life he didn't kiss me hello.

It sliced clean through the center of me and I froze. I understood.

Whatever version of him came back from Ohio wasn't ready for hugs or kisses. Not even for me. Yet.

I nodded, took his bag. I opened the car door and sat in the front seat like nothing had cracked.

And I drove my son home.

The ride was nearly unbearable. Mikey stared out the window and couldn't speak. Larry whispers to me: "He has been like that since the brain bleed from the SEEG diagnostic surgery."

I tried humor. I reintroduced myself like we were meeting for the first time—because that's how foreign he felt—but he didn't even blink at it.

He was still Mikey, but not *the* Mikey who made soundtracks out of breakfast, read to cats, sang to the dog and danced to microwave beeps making everything in our house hum.

Now?

Silence stuck to him like a second skin.

Once home, he sat curled in the corner of the couch, blanket tight around his shoulders, hoodie pulled low, eyes fixed on nothing in particular. Not even us.

Oreo rested his head on Mikey's lap, every so often looking up like he was checking to see if the lights were back on inside.

They weren't.

That night, I sat on the floor beside his bed. Not speaking, just... being.

His breathing was shallow, shoulders curled toward the wall.

I whispered, "Do you want me to sing?"

He didn't answer.

But after a long silence, I heard it.

"I don't know how to be me anymore."

My heart cracked in places I didn't know were still breakable.

I reached for his hand, just to let him know I was still there.

"You don't have to," I whispered.

"I'll remember for both of us."

~

In the prologue, I said that was the first time in twenty-one years he didn't kiss me.

This?

This was the first time I met the version of him that would need all of me, my patience, my belief, my brutal, exhausted, trembling love.

He came back, but he came back in pieces.

Loving him now meant learning to love the *after*…

Not just the memory.

Chapter 82

The Family Meeting

I've heard a lot of devastating words in war zones, courtrooms, and hospitals. But nothing hits like "There's nothing more we can do."

August, 2025. St. Augustine

The day before our telemedicine appointment with Ohio, that sentence kept circling my mind like a storm cloud refusing to break. I was dreading they would say the words no mother wants echoing in her kitchen, her chest, or her prayers.

"Not a surgery candidate. No new pills. Nothing we can do."

Hope had been quiet lately, but it hadn't gone anywhere.

When that familiar fire stirred—the same one that carried me through places and situations I never asked for—I knew exactly what I needed to do.

It was time for a family meeting.

In our house, "family meeting" wasn't just a phrase. It was a ritual—right up there with *Slava, sarma,* and the annual unpacking of ornaments we still pretend we'll store neatly next year. Family meetings marked big crossroads: moving countries, school changes, medical crises, and the time Oreo swallowed a sock, and I briefly wondered if we needed last rites. Mikey treated them like they were mission briefings and he was the commander.

I always go back to one of my favorite examples.

Summer 2016. St. Augustine

"Mom?"

"Yes, Curly?"

"When's the last day of school?"

I glanced at Larry, because questions asked in that tone only meant one thing.

"May 23rd… why?"

"Well…" Mikey said, dragging it out. "I was thinking… Maybe I could spend the summer in Europe. Again."

"Again?" Larry asked, raising a single eyebrow—which, in dad-speak, translates to: *I've seen this episode before.*

"Mmm-hmm." I nodded, "And you'd travel when?"

He didn't even blink. "May 24th"

I stared. "You mean the *very next day*? Like, toss your final exam in the air, high-five the janitor, and board a plane before the ink dries on your last multiple choice?"

He grinned.

Larry started laughing. I tried to scold him with my eyes, but even I couldn't hold it in.

"All right," Larry said, hands up in surrender. "Let's take a vote. Who's in favor of Curly leaving for Europe immediately after finals?"

Mikey raised both hands. And Oreos paws.

Larry joined him—traitor.

I shook my head. "Guess you're packing."

Summer 2025.

That intuition of mine... never faded.

This family meeting was about preparing Mikey for the likelihood that Ohio would say no again, and making sure he heard that word without losing heart.

I told him the truth: they might not have answers. It didn't mean *he* didn't have a future. It just meant they had reached the end of theirs.

What he didn't know was that I had kept going. I researched. I sent emails across continents. I made calls in the middle of the night. And during his stay in Ohio, I secured appointments with neuro-metabolic specialists in Europe who treat the *cause*, not just the symptoms. They might be blunt, overworked, and allergic to bedside manner, but I'll take harsh honesty and a correct diagnosis over a polite shrug in a white coat here any day.

Starting the race late doesn't change the finish line.

But this meeting—this messy, funny, beautiful gathering—reminded me that sometimes, *no* isn't a dead end.

Sometimes, it's just a sign pointing toward a better road.

Chapter 83

The Train in the Tunnel

They said, "We're out of options." I heard, "We're done trying."

I didn't even realize I had whispered,

"Are you sure? There has to be something," until the doctor repeated himself—slower this time, as if gentleness could soften the blow.

"Ma'am… there's nothing more we can do."

Nothing prepares you for hearing those words. Not even a thousand family meetings.

We've been in the middle of the tunnel for so long.

What we saw as light was only the glare of yet another train coming straight for us. We stood on the tracks, frozen in ours.

"Is this it?" I asked Larry, my voice barely staying steady.

He didn't answer right away.

"I… I don't know anymore," he finally said.

And in that silence, I knew the train had already hit us.

At night, I fall asleep with a chest full of "what ifs," only to wake up with the same weight pressing on my lungs. Once, I said them out loud to Larry in the dark.

"What if the first doctor hadn't rushed the wrong medication?"

"I don't know," he answered.

"What if inexperienced residents hadn't been making decisions meant for specialists?"

"I don't know."

"What if we hadn't gone to Starlight Children's?"

He swallowed hard. "I… don't know."

"What if CPS hadn't been weaponized against us?"

Larry closed his eyes. "I wish I had answers."

What if the only treatment that was working hadn't been taken away?

Have *you* ever worn those awful "what if" shoes? I did. Wore them for years. Got blisters and no answers.

Mikey is alive, but the boy he was? He's gone.

The one who remains carries the scars of battles he never chose.

One day, he asked quietly, "Why do I feel like my life stopped, Mom?"

I didn't want to lie. "Because someone stole moments you should've had," I said.

He blinked hard, looking away. "Will it ever come back?"

"I don't know," I whispered, "but I'm not giving up."

I mourn the future that was stolen from him, and some days, I wonder: *What if* God is punishing me for losing faith?

I am starting to forget what healthy Mikey looked like, the way his laughter filled up a room. The way he ran, arms open wide, so full of life.

Thank God for the millions of pictures I took. The moments I thought would slip away, even the little things, like when he went to the bathroom with a book in his hand.

Little did I know they'd be all I had left of the Mikey I was losing.

Two things remain untouched by restrictions: Sorrow. And faith.

This is not the ending we wanted for him, but it is not the end of his story.

~

Mikey's never been kissed. He's never been on a date (even Angela stopped texting after Starlight Hospital). College isn't even a thought. Those things break him in ways I can't explain. I can't comfort him. I can't fix this.

I lie awake wondering what will happen when Larry and I are gone.

I thought I knew how the world worked. This journey proved I didn't. It opened my eyes to truths I wish I could unsee—but here we are.

So, if I can offer anything, it's this:

Love fiercely.

Forgive quickly.

Hold your people close.

Because one day, it will be the last day.

And you might not even know it.

Chapter 84

Life After "We Can't Help You"

N*o one warns you that after the world stops ending, there's still a world left to live in—and it's nothing like the one you had.*

Mikey is home, but the days have lost their shape and folded into each other like smoke after a fire—thick, disoriented, impossible to separate. People spoke of "getting back to normal," as if normal were a place on a map, a town you could reach if you followed the right roads.

The fire burned the roads that led there.

We practiced small life, took walks to the mailbox. Drank coffee that stayed warm long enough to finish. Rinsed dishes without drama. Answered work calls in flat voices.

There was no joy.

On some nights, I swore I heard the guitar, even when no one touched it. The sound floated through the house like memory still had visitation rights. I didn't push it away: I stood still and let it move through me—like maybe grief could be musical, and the house could still remember what it meant to be full.

~

We are in our seventh season of heartache now. Grief changes shape, but it never leaves.

To date:

15,774 seizures (and counting).

43 ambulance rides.

38 hospital stays.

21 failed medications.

17 scars on his beautiful head.

Five intubations.

Two death pronouncements.

One encounter with Jesus.

Zero expectations.

That's what the surgeon told us before the last procedure. But Mikey—thirsting for the life he hadn't yet lived—said yes without flinching. And somehow, impossibly, frail and aching and stitched together like a question left unanswered, he came home.

Seventeen scars remain, each one a stubborn testament to how badly he still wants to be here.

But the fight cost him.

The boy who used to sing himself awake now moved through the house like a note with no instrument. Speech therapy began the day he couldn't finish a sentence. Thoughts fragmented like glass under pressure. Anger showed up, without knocking.

And joy? Joy stayed gone.

I watched my son go silent in the same house where music used to save him.

It felt like the whole world was losing sound.

Chapter 85

The Science of Staying

I *stopped praying for the world we lost. That grave has no headstone, but I visit it daily.*

He sat across from me on the couch, his silhouette suddenly unfamiliar. Ohio had taken his curls—those untamable, sun-catching spirals that once crowned him like a boy-king. Shaved clean for wires, probes, and promises. Tests that drilled for answers and returned with scarring silence. His scalp shone where his childhood used to live. It wasn't just hair that had been taken; it was a softness, a secret language we'd spoken without words. Now he looked older with suffering's overnight age.

He rubbed his bare head as if the curls might return under his palm. His body hadn't yet caught up with what it had lost. Then he said something I NEVER heard him say before–exhaustion stripped of costume:

"All of this makes me wanna give up."

I didn't rush to answer: confessions need silence to burn, and the only right thing to do is kneel beside them.

We sat in it together—his voice gone quiet, my heart refusing to follow.

"I don't have answers," I said quietly.

His jaw tensed, but he didn't interrupt.

"But I don't think giving up means what it used to."

He didn't look at me, but his shoulders lowered, just slightly.

"I keep thinking about how many discoveries almost didn't happen."

I took a breath.

"There are scientists," I said, "who failed hundreds of times. The world stopped watching, the funding dried up, but they kept going. They had *resolve*. They believed the cure might come one trial after the last collapse. That the breakthrough might be hiding just beyond the next try. They didn't quit, even when everything in them said they should. And one day, the answer came, because they stayed and kept trying. Maybe that's what faith is sometimes—just staying long enough to see what happens next."

He didn't look up, but his breathing shifted, small evidence of life answering life.

"You've been through so much, baby. And yes—Ohio said no, but that wasn't the end. It was just a *not this way*. Your brain isn't broken, it's beautiful. And we're not done searching."

I leaned closer.

"The next leg of the journey is different. We're looking now—not for another surgery, but for the right doctor. One who understands neuro-inflammation. One you will see in December, in Europe, who sees the full picture. Ohio gave us a verdict, but they don't get the final say. We're still writing this story."

I held his hands. "That's why you take voice lessons on Wednesdays, to reclaim sound—your sound—one note at a time. Just like a scientist running another experiment. *You're not done yet.*"

His eyes flicked to mine. Just briefly. "Do you *really* believe that?" he asked. "Do you *really* think someone else can help?"

And here—here is where I cracked. I nodded, too fast. My throat tightened.

"I *do*. And until we find them, we hold steady."

He didn't answer. But his breathing changed, like something deep in him remembered how to listen.

We started talking about our upcoming annual pumpkin-carving party. Friends would come. For a few hours the house would smell of cinnamon and earth and candle smoke instead of antiseptic. We would laugh with our hands sticky from seeds. That, too, was an experiment—a hypothesis that joy could still rise in a house like this.

But it was also proof that we're still here, still searching and softening the edges of hard days with little plans.

Almost without meaning to, I whispered the question that had been burning inside me, like Job under the weight of his ash heap: *"Why this fire, Lord? Why is his head shaved, his voice stolen, his future narrowed?"*

I whispered the same thing I whispered on that mountaintop in Ostrog twenty-two years ago: *"If this is the fire You've chosen for us, then please… make something holy from it."*

And somewhere beneath the silence I felt the answer—not an explanation, but a presence:

I am still here.

Chapter 86

The Scroll and the Sword

I *was born into a war I could not see.*
So was my son.

From the moment I drew breath, I lived inside an inheritance I had not yet learned to read. My family's memory sat in the rooms like the smell of bread—familiar, inviting, impossible to ignore. It was in the way my grandmother crossed herself before breakfast, in the way my grandfather folded his coat like a shield, in the silence that fell whenever a distant bell tolled. I grew up believing that living quietly was its own kind of courage.

History did not stop at my doorstep.

It came inside.

Inheritance of Fire

I wasn't the first to stand on the world's sharp edge: my ancestors had been doing it for centuries. On battlefields where the cross nearly toppled, they chose defiance over defeat. When blizzards buried the living and the dead, they kept moving—so relentless that commanders called them *"the army that refused to die."* When bullets tore through bodies, prayers still rose. When red stars tried to silence faith, my grandmothers lit candles anyway, their whispers louder than any regime.

This is the marrow I carry: psalms as shields, prayers as weapons, truth as survival.

The Scroll

The first time I heard my grandmother whisper about it, she didn't use words like destiny. She simply said, "When a child is born, two witnesses come. They carry scrolls. And on those scrolls, the story of that child is already written." For her, it explained why some walked through fire and didn't burn.

Her words landed like fire in my chest. I remember staring at my own hands and wondering: What did they write about me? Laughter, or loss? Light, or sorrow?

Looking back, I see how that quiet teaching shaped every choice I made: when to stay, when to leave, when to become invisible and when to stand.

The Unseen War

For years I thought those scrolls belonged to the dead, the sword to the past. I was wrong.

The war never stayed in books. It lived in basements where we sang louder than bombs, in kitchens where whispers became prayer.

And one day, it came for my son.

From the outside, he looked like any boy—curls that refused to be tamed, laughter that filled rooms.

An invisible enemy raged: seizures like storms, tests with no answers, doctors with more questions than cures.

He didn't fight with visible weapons, but with joy and faith that refused to bow. With light that refused to dim. I learned then: You don't have to be a soldier to be brave—you just have to refuse to give darkness the last word.

My son's illness did not feel heroic when it started, more like a slow theft. But the inheritance was never about glory. It was about showing up.

So, we kept showing up.

We prayed in hospital corridors and argued with insurance companies. We sang in churches and demanded MRIs. We set plates at tables and sat in waiting rooms until our knees went numb. We folded ourselves into the work of keeping a child alive, because love makes hard work holy.

Along the way, mercy showed up too: a doctor who stayed late to explain results, a neighbor who took him to a game so I could rest, a choir that sang by his bedside and made the machines sound less like verdicts and more like rhythm. Those mercies bent the arc.

This was the assignment: entrusted work. The same stubborn refusal my ancestors used to keep a faith alive was now given new purpose.

It would keep my boy alive in small ways—phone calls, studies read, prayers whispered at dawn.

It was the scroll, rewritten not in fate but in decisions: hold him, fight for him, sing for him, name him blessed even while naming the pain.

The same verses that carried my grandmothers through fire now wove themselves into him. Generation to generation. Bloodline to bloodline.

Suddenly, I understood: the scrolls had not cursed me. They had assigned me: She will be born into wars—old and new—and she will not break. Her son will fight an enemy no one can see, and she will not let him fight alone. When systems say no, she will say God. Her family's sword will not rust in museums. It will become a plowshare of prayer, carving life out of despair.

The Sword

If the scroll marked us, the sword forged us in prayer, persistence, and a love that refuses to quit. It taught us how to fight.

The battlefields moved, but the war remained—fields to corridors, trenches to waiting rooms, prayers to the edge of hell.

The enemy was still real.

So was our love that endured.

We keep tending the wound and keep singing into silence. Passing the candle from hand to hand.

Writing, in action, the story we want to read at the end of the day: that in the smallest labors, the fiercest resistances are born.

The scroll.

The sword.

The unseen war.

And this time, the enemy has *no* idea who it's up against.

Chapter 87

The Stage

I *should've turned back when the second soldier winked at me. The wink wasn't flirting, but meant: I could end you, but I won't.*

1992-1996. War in Bosnia

The road from Sarajevo to my hometown should have taken a few hours. It took four days.

Every checkpoint was a gamble—rifles raised, questions barked, papers demanded. The air itself felt armed, thick with suspicion. I learned quickly to keep my voice low, my eyes steady, my heart still. Somehow, through soldiers and barricades, I made it home.

But home wasn't home anymore. Neighbors watched each other too long. Men lined up for weapons. Whispers of loyalty and betrayal clung to walls like smoke. The streets buzzed like the air before a storm.

The day after I finally made it to my home town, the rally began.

The square filled fast—men shouting about protection, revenge, and rifles to defend our soil, our women, our children. Fear made them louder; anger made them certain. Every word tossed into that crowd caught fire.

I was twenty-one, barely back from college. My heart pounded—not with hatred, that much I knew—but with something else I couldn't hold down.

I stood at the edge of the square, unsure how I had gotten so close. The shouts blurred into each other, words becoming noise, rage becoming rhythm. Then someone shoved a microphone into my hand. Maybe it was a dare. More likely a mistake.

Either way, I found myself on the stage.

I don't remember climbing the steps, only the silence when I took the microphone.

My voice trembled, but I spoke. I had to. Something inside me—grief, memory, defiance—refused to stay quiet.

"You say you are protecting our loved ones," I said. "But the rifles you raise will be aimed at the people we grew up with, at neighbors we once shared bread with. At friends who sat beside us in school."

A ripple moved through the crowd.

"Traitor!" someone spat.

"You don't know what you're talking about," another snapped.

"Nobody in your family got killed! Get off the stage while you still have a home to go to!"

The boos rose like a wave, drowning my words. I felt them hit my skin like stones.

Still, I tried again. I wanted to scream back, to meet their rage with my own. My legs were shaking, and I understood—hatred can't be answered with more hate.

It would kill me twice.

So, I said the only thing that felt true.

"You raise rifles in the name of love," I cried, "but they will only make orphans of the children you claim to protect. If you raise those guns, you will be pointing them at your brothers. At your friends. Your own soul."

The crowd erupted.

Hands pushed me sideways. Someone yanked the cord. The mic went dead.

I stumbled down the steps and into the dark, the roar of the crowd chasing me into silence.

2018-Present. Battlefield in America

Decades later, I'm still in a war—but the battlefield has changed. There are no sandbags or soldiers, only quiet cruelty delivered by clean hands.

I now fight from another continent, in another language, as a mother caught in a polite kind of violence that hollows her Miracle Child with bureaucracy, indifference, with laws forged to silence rather than shoot.

The rifles still aim; they just sit behind desks now.

Back then, they told me love made me weak, and for a time, I believed them. But I've come to know better:

Love is the only weapon that survives every war.

Once, I stood on a stage and was booed for saying only love survives.

Today, I stand on a different one and speak again. I still refuse to kneel.

So…

Don't you dare lose faith. Your love *will* endure everything.

I don't know who's reading this.

I'm breaking the silence.

Chapter 88

Front Seat Revival

S*ometimes, life teaches you lessons in a car at 45 miles an hour, with a son who won't sing and a song that insists you do.*

October, 2025. St. Augustine

We were in the car the other day. No big conversation, just the road, air, and a thousand-mile stare I've come to expect from Mikey these days.

I turned on the radio to fill the silence, more for me than for him. My favorite song came on, and the lyrics crashed through the speakers like they had been waiting for me.

I don't know what came over me. Maybe spiritual caffeine, maybe a little trauma jazz. Maybe I'm just a problem—but I went *all in*. Sang every word like a woman auditioning for a band that didn't want her. Off-key, dramatic and dangerous. Steering-wheel choreography, exaggerated vibrato, one-woman revival at 45 miles an hour.

"Sing with me!" I laughed, eyes still on the road.

Mikey didn't sing, but for a second—just a second—I *swear* his eyes smiled. He paused, thought about it. Didn't hum, but he didn't look away either.

"Mom," he said, deadpan. "I don't know the lyrics."

"Then hum," I told him. "Fake it till you feel it."

From the back seat, Larry let out the long, slow sigh of a man who's been married long enough to know what's coming and still can't stop it. The sigh only achievable after years of marriage to someone who treats every red light like a stage cue.

"Is this the deluxe edition of the concert?" he asked. "Or just the standard Tuesday breakdown setlist?"

I didn't respond. I was too busy nailing the bridge.

"Do I need to print tour shirts: *'I Survived the Front Seat Revival?'*" He shook his head, glanced at Mikey, and stage-whispered: "I married an entire jukebox musical. No intermission."

My playfulness was contagious. Mikey's hand started tapping his knee, catching rhythm, and then he said:

"I really like this song."

And just for a second… there it was. His eyes smiled. That spark—quiet, blink-and-you-miss-it—lit up just enough for me to believe he was still in there, reaching.

He's still in there. Maybe not all the time, and maybe not in the ways I remember, but still reaching. Still listening. Still… *feeling.*

That was it.

He didn't break into song and, no, the skies didn't part. But for a few minutes, my son sat beside me—alive and attentive, letting a song about defeating death carry him somewhere softer.

In this life we've built from fragments and seizures and songs that come on at just the right time, a flicker is enough to keep going.

That's what we do now: we sing into the silence until it sings back. It wasn't a miracle, but it was *something.* I've learned to grab the *somethings* with both hands and thank God like I just won the lottery.

And if one day you see a woman dancing offbeat at a red

light, weeping while singing into her iced coffee, give her a wave. She's still fighting, still believing.

And as sure as the sun will rise–she will keep goofing off.

I'm pretty sure the Big Guy upstairs has had so many head-palm moments watching me sing like someone who should have stopped three verses ago.

In the rearview mirror, I caught them both—Mikey tapping his knee, Larry pretending not to smile. Me, mid-bridge, still off-key, still somehow holding the note like it might save us.

This fight—this long, brutal, beautiful fight—unleashed a strength I didn't know I had.

I believe that same strength lives in you, too.

Quiet and waiting, just needing a reason to rise.

The song kept playing as the light changed.

The road opened wide and I let the wind take the last of my fear.

For once, the world felt possible again.

I didn't know then that the road would end at a table, and that laughter would find its way home.

Prayer Full Of Bags

We used to say "bag full of prayers" every time we packed for another hospital, another town, another state that might—just might—have the answer.

As we prepared for a medical pilgrimage to Europe, chasing yet another miracle, the phrase didn't fit anymore.

It was no longer a bag full of prayers; it was a prayer full of bags now.

Somewhere between then and now, everything changed.

Every version of us has died and been reborn in some ICU waiting room. In some neurologist's office. In a court hearing. On the bathroom floor at 2 a.m. after a seizure that stole more than just time.

Larry changed.

From uniform to unshaven. From mission-ready to nowhere-to-go. From drinking to dropping to rebuilding. He's quieter now. Still. Different.

I changed.

From healer to patient. From adventure to stillness. From steady faith to losing it entirely, to clawing it back piece by piece. I hold it now, even when it burns.

Mikey… our Mustache Man.

From miracle baby to silent prophet. From belly laughs to barely whispers. From stealing hearts to watching ours break. Ancient and knowing eyes full of sadness and full surrender. Still saving people without saying a word.

Everything changed.

God never did.

Chapter 89

The Table of Three

I hadn't realized how far we'd wandered until the city reminded me who we used to be.

December 2025. Belgrade.

Cheapest tickets we could find (Larry still not working) were priceless.

Airport again. No wheelchair this time. No balloons bobbing, hair not curly but gray now. No friendly waves at the arrival terminal; busy lives have no time.

The light of the Serbian winter burned our Floridian lungs clean.

The stench of Belgrade immediately warmed up my shivered heart; I'm almost home. A few short hours until the lake house and until the family folded us into their arms.

The motherland lay before us, covered in snow, opening roads that had been closed to us for too many years. The familiar sound of church bells greeted us from the distance—slow and steady—as if they kept time for those of us who'd wandered through wilderness too far and for too long.

We made it!

Inside, the kitchen windows fogged from the heat. Strings of Christmas lights looped across the cabinets, their colors winking in the steam—red, green, gold, a little crooked and utterly perfect.

Baba waited with *burek* fresh from the oven.

My sister, her husband, and their two girls were bursting with excitement—no shortage of love or hugs in that house that always smelled like happiness.

The girls stared as if I'd stepped out of a bedtime story. They only knew me from video calls and their mother's tales, and now here I was—a tall, loud aunt who couldn't stop kissing their red cheeks. They squealed and hid behind their mother's skirt, half-delighted, half-unsure whether to run or laugh.

On the stove, beans simmered—thick, slow, patient—rich with garlic and oil, pulling memories out of hiding. I thought of all the years it took to love them again, to taste peace in what once tasted like survival.

Mikey perched by the window, tracing circles in the condensation, humming to himself the way he used to when life still tasted simple.

The embroidered tablecloth—faded from decades of washing—caught the light of the stove's small flame. It proudly held the chessboard Dad had set out for another duel with Mikey.

Icons glowed on the wall above it, their gold leaf trembling as the fire flickered and shadows prayed across their faces. The lake mirrored our faces as if remembering them from the last time we dared to visit.

We gathered around the table—fresh bread, a bowl of beans, a dish of apricots gleaming like coins between us. We ate. We laughed—because it *was* permitted.

My sister ladled more beans into my bowl. "Eat. You look like America doesn't feed you."

"America feeds me," I said. "But it only serves cold meals."

Baba waved her spoon like a gavel. "If you two talk more than you chew, I'm taking your plates."

"You've been saying that since 1989," my sister shot back, grinning.

"And still no one listens," *Baba* muttered—half laughing, half pretending not to.

Dad leaned back, chair squeaking, pointing at Mikey's full plate. "You'd better finish those beans, soldier. In my day we fought wars for less."

Mikey raised an eyebrow. "You also fought your neighbor over the TV remote."

"He started it," Dad said, deadpan—and the room burst open again. The table rocked under our elbows.

The Christmas lights blinked wildly as if laughing with us, casting patches of red and green across our faces.

My sister and I fell into that contagious laughter only sisters know—one feeding off the other until our sides hurt, until everyone else laughed at us laughing. Two goats bleating again, sharp and unladylike, scaring sorrow straight out of the room.

Mikey joined in, not knowing why—only that joy is contagious to those brave enough to stay near it.

For a moment, the world stopped keeping score. No hospitals. No prophecies. Only the steam rising, the beans cooling, the pulse of life carrying on.

Outside, the bells began again—distant, round, forgiving. We listened until their echo folded into our silence. And for the first time in years, the silence didn't ache.

We held hands, said our prayers, blessed the fasting feast before us, and ate until the waistlines begged us to stop.

Best. Christmas. Ever.

Maybe we laughed so loud because we knew what silence can take.

That night we didn't measure miracles—we just lived inside one.

And in that laughter, I felt the ache of every family still fighting their own long night, waiting for the morning.

Ours arrived; it didn't wear a coat of an answered prayer, but it kept showing up for us.

My eyes feasted on happy faces: *baba* snoring in the chair, dad arguing with the TV remote, Larry applying for jobs, Mikey puffing in the windows to draw hearts with Nadia's name.

Sister unglued the girls from my lap and took them to bed. My heart filled with unexplainable gratitude that overwhelmed me.

I've lived through three wars.

One in Bosnia.

One in the American health care system.

And one in the spirit realm.

Only one of them was ever acknowledged.

This is the story of all three. And we survived them all.

Outside, snow kept falling.

Inside, the beans cooled —

and love stayed warm.

The Last Candle

I light one candle and place it beside the icon on the mantle. The wax curls down the side like a slow, holy tear. The room smells like smoke, memory, and something like peace.

The same prayer I prayed at the monastery years ago won't leave me:

If there is still life in us, let it be used for something holy.

My body is tired and some days I carry pain like it's an organ. Some nights I bargain with time just to write a few more pages.

I don't know what tomorrow will ask of me, or how many more long hallways or long nights wait for us.

I know only this: The God who met me on that mountain has not stepped away from this house, and he held me in the nights I cried into the floor so Mikey wouldn't hear.

Mikey shifts in the next room; a quiet shuffle that says he's still here. Still fighting.

Still mine.

I whisper his name like I did the first time I held him.

I don't have an ending.

I have a Presence.

And for today, that is enough.

~

If I'm Not There When the Storm Breaks

My Final Letter To Mikey

Mikey,
My son.

When the world grows quiet in the places where my voice used to be and you reach for my hug but find only air—know this:

I didn't leave without loving you. I didn't go without watching you one last time through the eyes of a mother who never once regretted a second of your fight. I wrote our story so no one could silence it, not even time.

You were never the weight that broke me. You were the reason I stood with bones already cracked.

You were the scroll and the sword. The promise and the proof.

I don't know where the battle will find you next—in your body, your mind, or this loud, forgetting world—but I know this:

You have already survived what would have killed lesser men.

When they question your strength—let them.
You've already bled in silence and risen anyway.
If they try to box you in, break the box.
If they doubt your worth, remind them I raised a warrior.
If your knees hit the ground, let it be only to pray, then rise stronger.

And when the mirror shows you someone tired, someone unsure, someone who misses their mom more than they can say—
Smile anyway. That's when I'm closest.
That's how I'll know you made it through the night.
Don't let the sword dull. Don't drop the scroll.
And don't forget the sound of your own voice rising above the noise.

That voice?
It silences everything that tries to silence us.

I'll see you in the legacy you build.

Love,
Always —
Your Mama

I have fought the good fight, I have finished the race, I have kept the faith.
— 2 Timothy 4:7 (NIV)

Medical Glossary

Medications and Related Reactions

Depakote (Valproic Acid)

A seizure medication. In people who cannot metabolize it, Depakote becomes toxic and can trigger liver stress, confusion, agitation, worsening seizures, and high ammonia.

Allergy or Intolerance to Valproic Acid

When the body cannot break down valproic acid, it reacts as if poisoned. Symptoms may include behavioral changes, tremors, severe fatigue, vomiting, worsening seizures, and rapid neurological decline.

Dilantin Intoxication (Phenytoin Toxicity)

A dangerous buildup of Dilantin that poisons the brain. It can cause confusion, slurred speech, imbalance, tremors, or seizures triggered by the drug itself. Severe toxicity can leave temporary bright spots on brain scans that reflect brain intoxication.

Keppra Rage
A well-known behavioral reaction to the seizure medication Keppra. It can cause sudden irritability, intense anger, agitation, mood swings, or aggression that appear out of character and often come on without warning.

AED (Anti-Epileptic Drugs) Side Effects

Possible unwanted effects of seizure medications including dizziness, mood changes, memory problems, personality shifts, or increased seizures.

Rescue Medication

Fast-acting medication used during or right after a seizure to stop it from escalating into an emergency.

Infections and Inflammatory Conditions

Infections and Inflammatory Conditions

Bartonella (Cat Scratch Disease)

A hard-to-detect bacterial infection spread by cat scratch, ticks, or fleas. In severe or untreated cases, it can spread beyond the skin and lymph nodes and affect the brain, nerves, heart, and blood vessels.

Neurobartonellosis

A neurological form of Bartonella infection affecting the brain and nervous system. It can cause seizures, cognitive changes, pain, and neuropsychiatric symptoms.

Lyme Disease

A bacterial infection spread by ticks that can affect the brain, nerves, heart, and joints when untreated or misdiagnosed.

Die-Off Reaction (Herxheimer Reaction)

A temporary worsening of symptoms when antibiotics kill bacteria faster than the body can clear them. The inflammation surge can trigger seizures, pain, fevers, or emotional instability.

Black Mold Toxicity

Illness caused by exposure to toxic mold, often called black mold. It can trigger chronic inflammation, respiratory problems, headaches, neurological symptoms, fatigue, immune dysfunction, and in some cases seizures or cognitive changes.

Medical Crises and Emergency States

Status Epilepticus

A life-threatening emergency where a seizure lasts too long or multiple seizures happen without recovery. The brain is in a continuous electrical crisis. Without rapid treatment it can cause permanent brain injury, respiratory failure, or death.

Metabolic Crisis

A dangerous imbalance in the body's chemistry such as medication toxicity or high ammonia that can lead to confusion, seizures, or loss of consciousness.

High Ammonia

A buildup of ammonia in the bloodstream caused by medications or infections. It can lead to agitation, confusion, seizures, or neurological decline.

SUDEP (Sudden Unexpected Death in Epilepsy)

A major cause of death in epilepsy. A person can stop breathing or their heart can stop during or after a seizure, without warning and without a clear medical explanation. It is sudden, it is fatal, and it can happen even in children and young adults.

Locked-In Syndrome

A neurological condition caused by stroke or trauma where a person is conscious but cannot move or speak. Communication is usually limited to eye movements.

Coma (Post-Seizure Coma)

A profound loss of consciousness that can follow a severe or prolonged seizure. The brain becomes overwhelmed and shuts down normal responsiveness to protect itself. The person cannot wake, communicate, or respond, and may require breathing support.

Hospital Interventions and Support

Intubation

Insertion of a breathing tube to help a person breathe during a medical crisis.

Life Support

Critical medical intervention used when a person cannot sustain life on their own. This includes mechanical ventilation to take over breathing, medications that stabilize the heart and blood pressure, and systems that support failing organs.

Critical Neurological Care

Emergency-level treatment for life-threatening brain or nervous system crises. It includes continuous monitoring, rapid intervention, seizure control, management of swelling or injury, and support for breathing or vital functions when the brain is at risk. Patients in critical neurological care require immediate, specialized attention to prevent permanent damage or death.

Stress-Driven or Systemic Conditions

Broken Heart Syndrome (Takotsubo Cardiomyopathy)

A sudden, severe weakening of the heart triggered by extreme emotional or physical stress. It can feel and look like a heart attack, with chest pain, shortness of breath, and collapse. The heart's main pumping chamber temporarily stops working properly, often after trauma, shock, or profound grief.

Perfect Storm (Medical Context)

A combination of multiple factors (such as medical, biological, or environmental) that amplify each other and push the body into crisis. No single cause is enough on its own, but together they create a rapid, dangerous spiral that can lead to seizures, organ stress, or life-threatening decline.

Acknowledgments

To my God—

The Author of this story.

The One who knew the ending before I knew there was a beginning.

The One who writes in silence, waits through suffering, and bottles every tear like it's holy.

Thank You for trusting me with this war.

Thank You for trusting me with this child.

And thank You for never letting go—
even when I almost did.

This book is Yours.

To my husband, Larry—

My colonel who stood when I couldn't. Your patience, your pancakes—all miracles in their own right.

To my son, Michael Gabriel—

My scroll and my sword.

You made me a mother. You made me brave.

You made me get up when the world said stay down.

This book exists because you do.

To my parents, and to my sweet sister, Sladjana—

My anchor across oceans.

Your love crossed borders and time zones, holding me together when I was coming apart.

You were the bridge when I had no ground left beneath me.

To our acquired family in America—

You know who you are.

Thank you for showing up in the storm: for meals, prayers, beds, and arms. For saying *"I believe you"* when no one else would.

To Stanislav and Aleksandra Kravljaca, Jack Jones, Marylin Edwards, Nancy and John Fout, Stefanie and John Robinson, Kea and Steve Blalock, Mike Sanfilippo, the "Miracle for Mikey" prayer warriors, and every soul who prayed for our boy and helped in ways beyond imagining—

You were provision, laughter, relief—a reminder that we were never alone.

To every doctor, nurse, therapist, advocate and healer who stepped up and dared to stay when the world turned its face (especially our humble neurologist, S.A.)—

You were lanterns in long hallways.

You made space for miracles.

And yes, even to the doctors who hurt Mikey—

You became our unlikely teachers, the rough soil where mercy took root.

Fertilizer, after all, grows the most beautiful flowers.

Thank you.

Your presence in the storm was no accident.

To our community—St. King Milutin Serbian Orthodox Church, my Bible Study Babes, every pastor, priest, and friend who showed up when others walked away—

You were manna in the wilderness.
You prayed when I had no voice.
Gave when we had no strength.
Stood when we couldn't.
You held hope like it was your job.

To the readers—

You are *never* alone.
This is your song, too.
Light your candle.
Pick up your sword.

About the Author

Dr. Gordana Smith, DAOM, is the author of Book of the Silenced: a fearless work of literary nonfiction that confronts the moral, spiritual, and human cost of modern medicine when truth is inconvenient and suffering is dismissed.

A holistic primary care physician and the founder of Phoenix Rises Acupuncture, Dr. Smith brings rare authority to her writing rooted equally in clinical practice, lived trauma, and rigorous moral inquiry. Her work is shaped by a life marked by war, displacement, motherhood, and prolonged immersion in healthcare systems that too often confuse protocol with care. She understands the body not as an abstraction, but as a record of harm endured, resilience forged, and truths carried when language fails.

Book of the Silenced is not a retrospective memoir softened by time. It is a witness account written from inside the fire, composed between hospital rooms, legal battles, and moments where faith itself had to be interrogated to survive. With uncompromising clarity and lyrical restraint, Dr. Smith exposes the collision between institutional medicine and the sacred responsibility to protect life, while asking the questions most are trained not to ask: What happens when expertise eclipses humility? When systems protect themselves before the vulnerable? When silence becomes policy?

Her voice is exacting and unsentimental—at once clinical and prophetic—refusing both despair and easy redemption. Readers encounter a narrative that does not seek pity or absolution, but insists on presence, accountability, and truth. The result is a work that resonates deeply with clinicians, caregivers, parents, and anyone who has sensed that something essential has gone missing in the spaces where healing is supposed to occur.

Through both her medical practice and her writing, Dr. Smith advocates for those rendered invisible by power, process, and indifference. She believes healing begins when silence is broken, and that some stories, once spoken, permanently alter the landscape they enter.

Dr. Smith lives in St. Augustine, Florida, with her husband—a retired colonel and lifelong soldier—and their extraordinary son Mikey, known affectionately as "Mustache Man."

Together, they lead The MikeyAct, transforming private pain into public purpose and giving voice to those too often erased by systems meant to protect them.

This book is for those who stayed silent because they had no choice, and for those who will not be silent *ever* again.

www.ingramcontent.com/pod-product-compliance
Ingram Content Group UK Ltd.
Pitfield, Milton Keynes, MK11 3LW, UK
UKHW022002190726
13853UKWH00004B/1681